LOBSTER AT LITTLEHAMPTON

An Edwardian Childhood

Chapter 10, 'The Bellocs: Cautionary Tales', was first published by Harpers Magazine.

LOBSTER AT LITTLEHAMPTON

An Edwardian Childhood

Clare Sheppard

Illustrated by

Christina Sheppard

TABB HOUSE
Padstow

First published 1995

Tabb House, 7 Church Street, Padstow, Cornwall, PL28 8BG

ISBN 0 907018 94 7 hardback
ISBN 1 873951 17 5 paperback

British Library Cataloguing-in-Publication Data:
A catalogue record of this title is available from the
British Library.

Typeset by Exe Valley Dataset Ltd, Exeter
Printed and bound by Short Run Press, Exeter

CONTENTS

LIST OF ILLUSTRATIONS

This book was written by
Clare Sheppard for her grandchildren

MY FAMILY

A Summer Marriage

I WAS born on Michaelmas Day in 1904 with a caul over my face. There is a superstition that a caul is a talisman against drowning. My mother kept mine; but it was stolen, or so she thought, by a nursery maid whose sweetheart was a sailor.

There had been many upheavals for my parents at about that time and a third child must have seemed to them, by comparison, a matter of minor importance. My father had given up his post in the Ministry of Education to take up journalism, they had sold their house in London to settle in the country, and they had changed their religion. Their new home at Ford was on the Sussex coast, a few miles from Arundel where the great castle overlooks the river Arun as it curls its way to the sea. On the same hill stands a fine

1

church that was built in 1873 in Gothic style by the Duke of Norfolk on whose estate they now lived. It was here, in this romantic setting, that my father made his enthusiastic submission to Rome, my mother following him soon after with trepidation. Then it was her mother's turn to follow them. She was Blanche Warre Cornish, wife of the Provost of Eton College, and her conversion was quite a scandal. The people of Eton were used to her being eccentric, but this was going too far.

At the time my parents changed their faith English people were extraordinarily ignorant of Catholicism. Isolationism and a conviction of the superiority of the Anglo-Saxon race were prevalent, and though all educated people spoke foreign languages and toured Europe extensively, they did so without any sense of identity with the countries they visited. When the English convert travelled abroad he discovered that he had stepped into history, as if a great gulf separating him from the Middle Ages had been bridged and even classical times had come into clearer focus. He saw Europe with new eyes – from inside. It was an exciting experience.

But I must go back a little to speak of my forbears and shall begin with my mother's father Francis Warre Cornish, first an Eton housemaster, then Vice-Provost and Librarian. For several centuries his forbears had lived quiet lives as country squires in Devonshire and Somerset, intermarrying with local families, building nice houses, and producing a remarkably high percentage of clergymen. Perhaps he thought that those roots went deep enough; maybe he felt instinctively that it was time to bring a more dynamic strain into his line through the Ritchie family with its military and legal tradition, and a record of competent administration in the Indian Civil Service. He met Blanche Ritchie, daughter of the Advocate General of Bengal*, when staying at Lulworth for a holiday, and he married her in 1866.

It was said of her that when she heard of the young classical scholar who was staying in the same village, she posed herself in a bow window sitting in her crinoline and reading a book. Although she was only seventeen, it was not unusual for her to spend her time reading; she was a serious, intellectual girl of remarkable originality and later in life she wrote a great deal of literary criticism and a novel.

I don't remember my grandmother speaking of India, but she often referred to Paris where she spent part of her childhood staying with her Thackeray cousins. She told us how William Makepeace, when walking in the streets with her, made her take his arm: "Then everyone will think that we are husband and wife". His eldest daughter, Anne, was ten years older than her and was later to marry her brother Richard†.

As an old lady, Anne Ritchie, known to all her descendants and their relations as Aunt Anny, wrote some memoirs which give an idea of the cultural life in Paris in the 1850s, describing the glimpses that she had as a little girl of such figures as Robert and Elizabeth Browning and

---

*Sir William Ritchie.
†Sir Richmond Ritchie, Under Secretary of State for India.

poor Charlotte Brontë, so heavy on hand that William Makepeace was observed slipping out of his front door with his finger on his lips and a wink. She recalls Georges Sand saluting her grandmother from a box at the theatre with a sad smile and low bowing of her head; and Chopin, frail and exhausted after playing the piano all through the night, when she was taken to visit him one morning by an old lady who presented him with a basketful of delicacies that she had prepared for him. He was then living alone.

The two cousins, Blanche and Anne, in spite of their ten years difference in age, remained devoted friends throughout their lives.

After her marriage Blanche Warre Cornish was to be a frequent guest at Little Holland House and an habituée of Tennyson's home in the Isle of Wight. She was to have her children photographed by Mrs Cameron as angels reclining on clouds with wings pinned onto their backs and unhappy expressions on their faces and, like her cousin Anne in Paris, she was to meet in her own country most of the famous writers and artists of her day.

My paternal grandfather, Archibald Balfour, was the founder and director of the New Russia Co. and a merchant banker. The word 'staid' with its overtone of dullness is generally used to describe such families as the Balfours of Pilrig. They rose from being farmers to courtiers to the Kings of Scotland who gave them their lands, and they built Pilrig Castle; but their records are rather uneventful, except for one shining light. This was Sir John Harington, the inventor of the water closet, a poet whom Queen Elizabeth dismissed from her court for his unseemly conversation.

It is a tradition in the family to have his portrait in an appropriate place. They also have kinship with Robert Louis Stevenson whose mother was Margaret Balfour. It was to please a young cousin called David Balfour that he chose that name for the hero of *Kidnapped*.

Little of interest seems to have happened to the Balfours until my grandfather made a fortune in Russia. When, as a young man, he aspired to the hand of the pretty heiress Sophie Weguelin, her father Mathias Weguelin turned him down as a suitor and told him that he should first prove his worth. Weguelin owned tracts of arable land in the Steppe and he offered Archibald a post in the business and sent him safely far away to Russia.

On his travels Archibald Balfour met with a Welshman called Hughes who had discovered iron and copper in the Ukraine, and had begun to prospect. Hughes was in need of capital to expand his business and found himself up against many difficulties, one being the incapacity of the Russian peasant to turn to mining. Although a little town had sprung up around his mines, named Yousovka after him, the business was not prospering well. My grandfather persuaded Weguelin to sell his cornfields and buy Hughes's mines. This showed remarkable foresight. The steamship was making the import of Canadian corn possible at a highly competitive price. Mathias took Archibald's advice and gave him his daughter Sophie's hand.

The business was built up and modernised. It extended later to engineering and bridge building, and so prospered that it eventually paid dividends at the rate of 100%. My grandfather employed some trained miners from Wales and sent them out to Russia; terraced houses were built for them such as are to be found in nineteenth century industrial towns in England. Many Welsh names must have been transformed as Hughes's had been, and my grand-father's Lowland name was immortalised and russified when another little town sprang up nearby, to be called Balforka. It is said to be a horrid little place, but the family should be as proud of it as of Pilrig Castle.

Later the name Yousovka changed to Stalino and after the de-Stalinisation to Donetz. It must now be one of the largest industrial centres in the USSR. It would be interesting to know if it has a Balforka Street. When Krushchev came to London and was driven through the East End, he was overheard by an interpreter to say to one of his retinue "Those are like the houses that Balfour built at Donetz". So Archibald is still remembered there, if only as a ruthless exploiter of slave labour.

My father was Reginald Balfour, the youngest of Archibald's seven children. He was born and educated in

London, being a Queen's scholar at Westminster. He lived in the school while his four elder brothers who were 'townsmen' went there daily, in top hats in the family carriage and pair. His two sisters and four brothers were all clever, handsome and vigorous, but he was the cleverest, winning a scholarship and a double first at Cambridge. At Cambridge he shared rooms with Gerald Warre Cornish and there met his younger sister, Charlotte, who was to be my mother.

In the summer of 1898 Charlotte and Gerald went to stay with the Balfours at their shooting lodge in Sutherland. Writing as one classical scholar to another, Gerald made elaborate plans for their journey, in hexameters scribbled on the back of a post card:

> Yes, I think we must come, my sister and I, to the Highlands.
> We shall arrive, I expect, by sea from Bristol to Glasgow.

and so on, ending:

> I am forever, dear Reggie, your most affectionate Gerald.

That holiday in Scotland led to what was then known as an 'understanding' between Reginald and Charlotte – a situation so hard to imagine in the light of present day custom that I think it will be best conveyed by excerpts from my grandmother's diary which is a period piece, written with rather the same mentality as her occasional comments on current events such as Mafeking or the Dreyfus affair.

October 30th, 1898. Radiant morning after the rain. Whilst finishing dressing before breakfast, I thought I saw married lovers come from the trees at the end of Fellows' Eyot*. They came into the open and I recognised Chartie and Reggie, both hatless, very tall, with faces turned to each other. I did my best to take the view of 'friendship'. I thought that Reggie wished to commend it to me too by his gentleness, by his own special:

> Parlare in modo soave e benigno
> Qual non si senta in questa mortal marca.

Christmas Eve, 1898. When I found Char in her room she had received the night before a letter of despondency. Reggie had tried to find some *via media* between what had been and what she said must be final, but she had told him all must be at an end.
December 26th, 1898. Maurice [Baring] arrived at eleven. Edith [Sichel] came for dinner. Superb games in evening.

They were both very young; he was still at Cambridge; there were doubts about his delicate health (a tumour on the brain had been suspected!); his profession had not been chosen; the Cornishes could only offer a small dowry; and the Balfours were against the match.

There was further agitation when Reggie first considered joining the church of Rome. During this crisis Maurice Baring, who was later to become such an enthusiastic Catholic himself, wrote to Charlotte:

Padlock,
My dear beloved Scarlet red Tomato, be at ease, there is *no* likelihood of Reggie becoming an R.C.
    Yrs M.B.

*Probably the Old English word *eyot*, pronounced 'ait', meaning a small island, especially in a river.

The agitations and agonies were incessant, but by the end of 1899 things seemed to have calmed down a little.

December 1st. Went to Cambridge. Char's April looks that day and R's face as he looked at her I never can forget.

Chaperoning was very strict. There was no question of Charlotte going to Cambridge alone and there are long letters from Reggie making plans for May Week with the enlistment of a team of mature ladies. When they went to Durham for Gerald Cornish's ordination under the Vice-Provost's escort, the journey involved spending the night in an hotel at Peterborough. There is an entry: 'R and C had a long walk returning at eleven after dinner greatly to Frank's despair.' This would have been a culpable infringement of the rules. Fiancés counted themselves lucky if they managed to be alone together for any length of time, especially after dark. But there is a later entry: 'How desperately unnatural is the engagement time on looking back.'

It would seem that by March 20th all had been settled:

Season of the thrush, season of the bright spiritual light and invigorating wind. Hail the last day of Winter, tomorrow Spring will be here; every soul is out energising, athleticising, but I am alone in the collegiate garden; the elms are a red tangle of park beyond the red wall. San Ambrogio [Ambrose the gardener] has just planted two cypresses for me. Tomorrow is the first day of Spring; begin sowing for the bridal.

Then she tells of spending the morning in the garden with Reggie and Char, 'with their *vita nuova* breaking on every tree in thousands of blossoms.' Next, of an exquisite morning with cuckoo singing and Duggie Balfour and Reggie arriving in the evening 'in time to march with the school in torch-light procession to the castle. Scene in school yard more beautiful even than at the jubilee.' She goes to London to choose wedding presents and to see Eleanora Duse acting in *Magda*. Then comes the description of a horrific experience:

June 16th. Railway collision at Slough after happy morning choosing R's pearl tie pin, and Char's sapphire ring. I had so enjoyed doing this out of the fee for my 'Portraits and Prints' from *Pall Mall* magazine. Racing men filled the first class carriage with me. The bright June light fell on their wholesome faces.

At Slough an express train ran into the one that she was in:

Every window was shivered and the last batch of carriages was annihilated . . . one of the sporting men lay dead in a first class carriage in front of us. The whole time that our compartment was heaving up and down like a boat on a high sea, I was thinking 'Unkilled if only wounded, the wedding must not be stopped.' I then kept trying to remember where one ought to put one's legs. Arthur Coleridge was screaming on the floor.

She called imperiously: "Get up Mr Coleridge . . . Charlotte shall be married. Get up Mr Coleridge."
    She goes on:

I remember little terror. Only when all was over one felt faint. The look of unutterable thankfulness on the young faces I shall never forget; the young men were uplifted into angelic beings with delight at safety. So odd to see angelic radiance suddenly on young sporting faces! Mr Coleridge kept on thanking God. I had no inclination to do so, but a strong sense of the Unseen was upon me and I could not help making the sign of the Cross.

By this time, Reggie was already calling her 'Belle Mère' and plans for the wedding were in full swing. The diary is resumed on June 30th. 'Reggie arrived hatless on Fellows' Eyot with a magnificent pearl necklace in his hand. Maurice

and I had gone to heaven for a little bit on Romney Island but Mr Clarke arrived and brought us plumb back to earth.'

I must explain that Mr Clarke was a clergyman and Grandmama disliked clergymen and schoolmasters in general. Next she speaks of an atmosphere of presents and gatherings of Reggie's relations, Balfours, Talbots, and Lytteltons: 'Quartets on the leads. Jack Talbot's voice sad and grim. May's and Char's rising, beautifully undulated. So heard the moon in thinnest sickle rising over the beech trees on Fellows' Eyot.'

Oddly enough by the time we come to the wedding, the sunshine is less brilliant and there is a good deal of rain. Maurice comes to stay and they have a committee meeting about the wedding. 'Immense thought bestowed on the proper spot for Mr Balfour's hat and umbrella.' There were, however, clearings for 'Morning talks with Maurice under the lilac,' and when Reggie comes, he crosses the river instead of taking a cab from the station; 'Maurice is hiding to take him by surprise. It all failed. They were perfectly delightful.'

Then there comes an entry headed 'On the Eve' – when the moon rose and 'every cloud seemed swept from the sky by the strength of her beams'. The wedding must have had a large attendance as the guests seem to have spread all over the school buildings: the College Hall, the Library, the Audit Room and Election Chamber, not to mention the Vice-Provost's house in which the rooms were large.

Morning resplendent. We feared heat and closed shutters in drawing-room whilst Reggie and Lord Lytton went on the river. Arranging presents was something large. Mrs Balfour and DD arrived and Mary Lyttelton with faithful Flora, all looking like roses, and went up to the bride lying on her bed amid her diamonds and pearls, her bridal dress over a chair. I then found myself with a bouquet walking to chapel with Anny*. Reggie soon came with his best man, both perfectly charming. The brides-maids waited in the ante-chapel looking like dryads. The radiant light fell through the windows on the stone never more solemnly. At last the bride came with her tall bunch of lilies looking beautiful on Frank's arm. The John Talbots were opposite me. Edmund Gosse in the stalls. When we sat down for a ponderous discourse by the Reverend the Honourable Edward[†], one could look about. The Neville Lyttons were just behind me, and Eddie Marsh. Mr and Mrs Balfour opposite, and Tom [Balfour] with tall figure and charming face. DD keenly interested – very Hera-like as usual. After the Vestry emotion I came out into the sun beneath a deep blue sky and saw Charlotte on Reggie's arm attended by her page, Oliver Lyttelton[‡], disappearing into the cloister. When I got to the College Hall, Edmund Gosse came up to the gallery with me and looked down on the scene below. Reggie caught sight of me from the dais where Chartie was cutting the cake attended by their 'best of men', Lord Lytton, who looked very handsome, but R was the handsomest of all. He smiled brightly to us and drank my health.

Anny came up into the gallery too and asked Edmund Gosse if it was not a wonder that so much sunshine and happiness came together in one hall. He replied that all would have disappeared tomorrow.

At length the bride went to change her dress and all moved to the garden and across Fellows' Eyot to see the departure.

And so they were married and went away in a punt to take a train from Datchet to Woking where they reached 'the sweet Hurst with all its lilies in flower'.

*Thackeray's daughter Lady Ritchie.
[†]Edward Lyttelton, Headmaster of Eton.
[‡]Later Viscount Chandos.

My grandmother continued that evening: 'Our own dear college garden was a triumph of Margaret's forethought, her roses and lilies were in perfection. The night was the finest I ever saw in England with brilliant moonlight.' Never so many lilies and roses, never such radiant sunshine nor such a brilliant moon as on that wedding day, July 10th, 1900.

FORD

Fragmented Pure Memories of Childhood

MY first memory is of foxgloves. I find myself in what seems a forest of them and am suddenly overcome with fear. Hester and David are picking off the petals to put onto their fingers and Nana is beyond them; a large woman in an apron, strange to me, is with us. I suddenly feel separated from my family as they penetrate into the deep forest leaving me with the strange woman who begins to fit some petals onto my fingers to amuse me. All at once, the foxgloves become malevolent creatures surrounding me on all sides and swallowing up my brother and sister and nurse. I am in a nightmare world and possessed by terror.

The strange woman takes me indoors, crying, and into one of those Victorian lavatories with a mahogany seat and patterned bowl of blue china. It ought to be a place of

15

comfort, but here I raise my voice and yell until Nana comes to the rescue. This must have been at Ford where there were so many foxgloves in the summer. I remember my sense of frustration at not being able to talk and I must have been about two years old.

In my mother's album there are many photographs of Ford: a snapshot of Hester sitting on the grass and whistling against a background of foxgloves, the perfection of a little girl with a halo of fair curly hair; David, also sitting among foxgloves under a mass of dark curls looking serious and remote; then I make my first appearance with my hair hanging in rat's tails and a tear on my cheek, angrily pulling a foxglove to pieces. Stephen, in his first sitting-up photograph, supported by Nana's hand, is seen fingering a foxglove with intense concentration.

The next memory is going down the wide oak staircase at Ford with David and Nana, one tread at a time, and we are called to from the landing above. Looking up I see a white ghost-like figure leaning over the balustrade waving and talking to us. It is my father in a white garment of some sort with a bath towel wrapped round his head. It takes me some time to realise who it is, but even after I have recognised his pale handsome face, I can't answer to his salutation. There has been a metamorphosis but the ghost is still part of him – it hasn't vanished as a ghost should. It so happens that my earliest impressions are of fear.

At Ford there was a lane to the side of the garden that led to the sea, and here I remember being in a pram with Stephen. At first I am possessed with anger at having been picked up and away from the company of Hester and David to be relegated to the lower regions of the nursery; then my anger dissolves under the sway of a much greater passion – fear again. I am surrounded by a flock of sheep panting and hustling and making the pram sway as they press against it. The voice of a vindictive nursery maid is heard as in a dream saying "There you are Clare. I told you so."

Another early memory is of being in a bathing hut on wheels by the sea. Nana had undressed me, and I was waiting to be taken down the steps when I saw David in a striped bathing dress on the sand and watching the sea trickling up over his feet. Suddenly a tall young 'boy' (it was really my mother) wearing what looked like knickerbockers and a red cap, strode up to him, picked him up to carry him out into the sea and dip him in the water. I was so petrified that I was unable to scream.

Then I saw the boy stand David up, and as he ran back to the shallow water I gasped with relief. The boy then began to swim sideways to me, rolling up and down on the swell of the waves. I must have been familiar with the Edward Lear Nonsense Book because he reminded me of a 'young person of somewhere' in a recumbent position. I was well away into a world of fantasy by now, and when the boy waved to me, smiling with Mother's smile and called to me in her voice, I was incapable of recognising her. David had nearly been drowned by an extraordinary creature; that was real and would remain real whatever the creature turned out to be. It was the same as with my father on the stairs – a figure in white with a bandage wrapped round its head was not less frightening because it turned into Daddy, but more so. The sight of my mother swimming must have made a deep impression on me. When I was older I had a dream about some brown naked creatures swimming side-stroke in the brackish water of a gutter, and whenever I heard the 'Hail Mary' recited and it came to 'Blessed art Thou amongst women', the words 'amongst women' conjured up a vision of them 'among Swimmin'. 'Swimmin' was the name of the creatures in my dream.

Ford Place was a beautiful Queen Anne house near Arundel, close to the Sussex coast. It stood high and square with a little walled garden in front led up to from the road by steps with a mounting-block to one side. My parents discovered panelling under plaster in several of the rooms and one or two fine mantelpieces, also hidden. The garden in which we played was full of variety and surprises; it was surrounded by high walls with arches and gates – each leading to a new world. The nurse, whom we adored and called Nana, was tiny and plump and looked like Mrs Hippo with very kind eyes. She had the faith and piety of the Irish peasant, the humour and the moodiness, but a caustic wit of her own. She left my mother at one time, as the babies followed in rapid succession, but came back later, saying "Sure the Devil you know is better than the one you don't." She had a laugh with real mirth in it that shook the whole of her body as she threw her head back. She used to tell us that she was the most beautiful woman in the world and would one day marry a millionaire, and Hester never knew if she should believe her: "You're *not*, Nana," she would say, "Mother's beautiful." I much regret there is no photograph of Nana – only of her hand supporting Stephen's back; but how well I remember Nana's hands –

lying in her plump little lap as she sat saying the rosary in a moment of leisure, clapping them together to call us in to tea from the garden, or holding a basin under my head during a bilious attack. They were gentle ministering hands that gave one a sense of security.

For my parents the years at Ford were intense and formative. Their new faith opened a whole world to them. It cut them off intellectually from their two families, but this gave their new friendships a special bond. The isolation of the English convert of their generation is hard to imagine now; a conversion was still looked upon as something akin to treachery, and was often punished by disinheritance. They turned part of the cellar at Ford into a chapel in which Mass was said by the priests who came to stay as their guests.

They had some remarkable neighbours, many of whom became lasting friends. There was Hilaire Belloc at King's Land near Horsham, already noticed as an author of promise – a young man of great exuberance and spirits, happily married with small children. About then he was as much engaged in politics as in literature. He and his friends the Chesterton brothers, Gilbert and Cecil, had their own printing press at King's Land which was used for their Liberal pamphlets as well as for the literary work of other writers of their circle such as Maurice Baring. Another frequent activity at King's Land was the bottling of wine sent from France in barrels. In this Belloc was sometimes joined by the young Winston Churchill.

A house not far away called Crabbet Park was the home of Neville and Judith Lytton. My mother described the

Lyttons to me as an immensely energetic couple, rising early to exercise on the Sussex downs Arab horses that had been bred from her father's stud, then spending several hours practising real tennis with their French instructor. They also devoted much time to the arts of poetry, painting and music. Neville played exquisitely on the ivory flute and was interested in the current revival of folk dancing.

Judith Lytton's father Wilfrid Scawen Blunt lived nearby at his Jacobean house Newbuildings Place. A poet, champion of the Arab cause, and founder of a famous stud which revived the stock of the Arab horse, he spent the winters at his house near Cairo, making frequent excursions into the desert on camels, often accompanied by his wife Lady Ann.

The Wilfrid Meynells settled at Greatham near Pulborough, he being an editor and journalist, and she a famous poet harbouring another poet – the drug-addicted Francis Thompson – and gathering many others round her, chief among them Coventry Patmore.

Surrounded by these several intellectual conclaves, what more interesting neighbours could my parents have had? There was the euphoria of new friends, new interests and new enthusiasms. But the promise of it all was not to be fulfilled.

My father died, taking his own life when in a state of acute depression, in the summer of 1907. I was two years old at the time so I cannot give an authentic account of him. Those who knew him all speak of his great charm, gaiety and high spirits. During the brief seven years of his marriage, he was to change his profession several times because of a recurring depressive illness. This quotation from his obituary gives an idea of some of the many qualities appreciated by his friends:

There was a poetry throughout his whole nature and it showed itself in his literary judgements and writings as well as in that keen realization of the drama of life which stimulated him to help his fellow men. A wonderful joyousness, a radiance, a youthful freshness of mind left their stamp even on his most serious work. He gave zest to any enterprise with which he was connected.

Typical of his enthusiasm was his devotion to St Francis of Assisi. He used to help the Franciscans on their annual camping mission to the hop pickers during the hop harvest.

In 1907, the year that my father died, we moved from Ford to 26 Church Row in Hampstead. It was here that I have a strange memory of finding myself in the hall, a Punch and Judy showman calling outside. His cry filled the street with an atmosphere of pantomime. I didn't want to go out to see him but I wanted to share my enthusiasm with someone else so I opened a door, to find- myself in a study where Uncle Tom Balfour was talking with my mother. I had the impression of interrupting an intimate conversation and of being an intruder; but I told them about the man in the street who was saying "'orby, 'orby" (Toby, Toby). Uncle Tom then picked up a metal paper weight in the shape of a spider, stooped down to my level,and recited 'Little Miss Muffet' to me. I was delighted. I knew that I was Miss Muffet and the spider was mine – there was something special about the spider and me, and it seemed to be a satisfactory answer to my confusion about the Punch and Judy show. A grown-up had entered into my inconsequent childhood world – but Mother was standing in the background and though she was smiling I felt that she wished me away.

I am aware of my mother in my first years as a slim graceful figure moving away from me with a sad smile on her face – all the more tantalising because of the look of sympathy in her dark eyes. Again, in the same house: I was sitting in my high chair in a room on the ground floor with the door open, and there was a sudden commotion. A man went down the basement stairs, opened a door at the bottom and began to talk in a loud voice. A few moments later a stout maid in a white cap and apron rushed up to our room to throw herself onto a sofa and rocked herself backwards and forwards, crying hysterically. At this I began to cry too, which started Stephen off. The din brought Nana back, and she said "Tut-tut," to the maid, who got up from the sofa and recovered herself, wiping her eyes on the corner of her apron. She came up to me and said something about a nice little 'bibie'. She and Nana stood on either side of me, telling me about a little baby. I didn't understand them, but the awful sobbing had stopped, and Nana's comfort was glowing round me so I went on with my tea. They were probably telling me of the birth of my third brother Christopher. He only lived for a few days. Stephen and I were taken up to see him; the room was rather dark, and Mother was lying flat on her back. The monthly nurse, called Linley, was standing up and spoke as though she knew us both intimately. I resented this as I had never seen her before; nor did I like the evident intimacy between her and Mother. I would have preferred to see

Mother standing and in command. I never liked to see Mother sideways. Stephen and I, just turned two and three years, stood on tiptoe to peer over the side of the cot; the baby's head was a small dark splodge on an expanse of white linen.

During the short time that we lived at Hampstead, Granny Balfour used sometimes to come in her carriage and pair to take us with her on her daily afternoon drive. Catte the coachman was our great favourite. He looked magnificent up aloft in his livery with a footman beside him, and we were proud of his friendship. It was at about this time, and rather later than most people, that our grandparents changed their carriage to an electric car, before having one with a petrol engine.

We were very excited and ran about the house, saying "Granny's got a motor, Granny's got a motor!" but when it arrived to pick us up I didn't recognise Catte, turned chauffeur, as he stood at the door with a rug over his arm. What a come down! No more topboots or cockades. He looked like anybody else in the long navy blue coat and the cap that came over his eyes.

The electric car went round and round the park silently at a snail's pace with Granny in a bonnet lined with dove grey chiffon and held by a ribbon that was tied in a bow to one side. She lay back on her cushions and talked to us in her gentle voice; and many other cars were doing the same for solitary old ladies – rich Victorian old ladies looking, some of them, rather wicked as they went round the Park in their motors, as they had done in their carriages, out of sheer force of habit. I can remember one in an electric car like Granny's, dressed all in purple, who gave me a look of real hatred, or so I felt, as she passed.

When I was four my mother took me to stay with her sister and brother-in-law, Molly and Desmond MacCarthy*, at their house, The Green Farm, in Suffolk. It was the first time for me to go away without Nana and to have Mother to myself, but that visit was an agony. I ate in the dining-room with the grown-ups and felt quite bewildered by their conversation. On two successive days Mother and Aunt Molly each had a fit of choking, and at every meal I dreaded it happening again – the choking was terrifying. Then there was Rachel, an infant in arms, who was inclined to be sick, and two dreadful dogs – a spaniel called Beau and a Prince Charles called Tasso (a breed being revived at that time by Neville Lytton) who charged at me and nearly knocked me down. I spent the afternoons with the MacCarthy nanny pushing the eldest child Michael in his pram about the village. She told me that the spots on his face came from the bites of some horrible creatures called mosquitoes and said suddenly "Look, there are some!" When I asked her where, she pointed with her finger saying "Look, there." I looked where she had pointed and saw a pair of striped socks hanging on a line in a cottage garden. Those were the horrible mosquitoes – and I

---

*Desmond MacCarthy (1877-1952), literary journalist. He wrote: 'Very young children take everything literally. Their interpretation of things and events, however fantastic, is more real and much more satisfying to them than the world of reality and facts. Spoken words, which may have differing spellings and different meanings though pronounced the same, have only one meaning for them – the one they first learnt.'

imagined them spreading their wings, like giant wasps, and hovering round Michael's face to bite it. I didn't feel happy at The Green Farm!

A few months later the MacCarthys came to stay with us. One day as we were finishing our tea, Hester got down and said "Now I am going to talk to my little girl." I glowed with pleasure at the thought of such attention – I loved being called 'little girl'; Nana used to smile at me with approval sometimes and say "Nice little girl". But, to my horror, Hester ran round the table on tiptoe (an affectation of hers) and went to the sofa on which little Rachel lay spread in her robe of many tucks, and I was overwhelmed with jealousy and disgust. What could Hester find to enjoy in that little baby who was liable to be sick at any minute?

The MacCarthy's nanny was called Millie; she was young with golden hair and a slightly cockney (Suffolk) accent, and after Dermod was born, she was joined by a nursery maid called Eva. Nana managed the four of us Balfours

single-handed. Perhaps she was a bad mixer and preferred to be on her own, for it was unusual then; but we must have had occasional nursery maids because I can remember several at different times – two of them having the name of Annie. One of these Annies was with us at our grandfather's house at Eton; she was pretty and used to cut bread by holding the loaf against her stomach drawing the knife towards her. We liked her very much, but she fell ill of a sick headache which sounded to me of all illnesses the most horrific, and I used to hurry past her door at the thought of her lying on her bed with such a revolting complaint. The other Annie I remember at our Balfour grandfather's house. This Annie smelt, and I complained of it in front of her. After my bath Nan insisted, in spite of my protests, that Annie should escort me back to the nursery, and the poor girl had to take me down a long passage crying loudly and stopping now and again to retch. Granny Balfour was walking laboriously on her stick at the end of the passage and gave me a look of reproof as we passed her, but I could see that she was amused. It was all very well for Granny! She wasn't so near to Annie as I was. After Annie had left us Nana asked me what she had smelt like, and my answer was "Annie smells like a flower." I meant that she smelt in the way that flowers do – strongly and with an individual scent, but I didn't explain, so Nana interrupted her sewing to throw her head back and have a good long laugh.

Sometimes I used to wish disloyally that we had a smart young nurse such as we met with some of the children we played with; but I never envied the MacCarthys their Millie and Eva. They seemed vulgar compared with our Nana and – horror of horrors – they even had boy-friends to whom they alluded as "my friend". I felt that children were entitled to the exclusive affection of their nurses, and when Nana showed me the photograph of a child that she had "reared", as she put it, I was astounded and couldn't imagine her looking after any children but us. Indeed when she did leave us she hadn't the heart to take on another family and went instead to her sister in Brussels to help her keep a lace shop.

Millie and Eva both married, but Millie waited till the children were old enough to do without her.

The Warre Cornish's nurse was another Eva, and she used to come to see my mother sometimes – a tall thin woman with spectacles and a mass of grey hair piled up on her head.

The older Balfour family's nurse was called Ann Cook. She was small, with masculine features – a heroic woman who went on the long journeys to Russia and back with our uncles and aunts when they were children. She had particularly loved my father and, to the end of her life, she saved money from a tiny pension with which to give us presents. These chaste dedicated women were to be found in nearly every family and asked for no reward for their sacrifices. It was taken for granted. But when Nana died my mother paid tribute to her by having engraved on her tombstone 'She was a devoted nurse', followed by the text 'Her children shall rise up and call her blessed.'

ETON

Warre Cornishes

MY grandmother has been remembered by several generations of Etonians for two things; first for a remark addressed to a lady after a reading of one of Molière's plays: "How wise you were not to *attempt* the French pronunciation"; and secondly for leaving a baby in the arms of an Eton boy on the platform at Windsor station. She went to the bookstall to choose something to read, became absorbed in an article, and got onto the train forgetting the baby. I tell the story as posterity has it, though I don't believe it to be accurate in detail.

She was famous for her unpredictable remarks. A friend once said, very aptly, that her mind worked like the knight's move on a chessboard – two squares forward and one sideways jumping over the other pieces. She seldom gave a clue to her train of thought and seemed to be darting from a mysterious world of her own, like a rocket from the sky, leaving her hearers bewildered yet strangely stimulated.

"Ah yes, Margate," she said when the resort was mentioned in the course of conversation, "a lot of people go there;" then lowering her voice and with intensity, "but they mustn't be disturbed." She didn't explain that she often went to Margate herself to write in peace and quiet or to recuperate from illness.

Sometimes her short compact sentences would be poetic. When looking at a thirteenth century statue of a smiling Virgin and Child, she said spontaneously to the Child who caresses a bird: "Enjoy your creature." When understandable they were illuminating: "Christianity – so complex – so ironical." They were often fierce: "The black crow mates for life," – addressed to an attractive young lady who was enjoying a flirtatious conversation with the Vice-Provost, – and "Nice, yes, if you are an admirer of the nice." Her crushing remarks are the most quoted, but she was very often encouraging and sympathetic. When a little girl was thrust into the drawing room crying from reluctance and embarrassment, she exclaimed "In tears, how becoming!" What better way of drying a child's tears?

Once when the three Tennyson boys (great grandsons of the poet) had been invited with their parents to lunch at The Cloisters, they arrived, five strong, to find her standing in the hall surrounded with luggage and drawing on her gloves with her eyes shut. She opened them for a moment and said abstractedly: "I'm just off to Italy," then, as an afterthought, "you will find some biscuits on the sideboard."

For her the things of the mind had to come first and, in their favour, practical considerations were often ignored. It was almost laudable, and certainly forgivable, to miss a train on account of a beautiful sunset. Speech was not to be defiled by the commonplace or the superfluous. Children have a fatal tendency to the banal and she would correct this in us constantly. We were allowed a great deal of freedom, but when we went into the drawing-room a high standard of civilised behaviour was imposed. 'Earth, air, fire, and water' was a game that she liked to play with us. She threw a wool ball with flashing eyes to each in turn and, as we caught it, we quickly had to name a creature that lived in the named element. The only animal that lived in fire was said to be a salamander. We were made to sing French and German songs to her accompaniment, after having the meaning of the words explained. Sometimes we were made to read books beyond our understanding. "Yes, you know David," she would say, placing him in a special armchair in order to read to him, "Mr Robert Browning once sat in that chair". A blank look would descend on David's face. Who could Mr Robert Browning be?

The common things of daily life were ennobled by their relation to some historical character. "Lobster at Littlehampton is classic," she asserted during a seaside holiday, going on to explain how Sir Hubert Parry liked to eat lobster after sailing on the Arun. By association the lobster on the table became a sacred beast to her, obliterating the commonness of the Littlehampton villa she rented, but she didn't think of telling us who Sir Hubert Parry was, nor did we ask.

There was a ban on comic papers at Eton and the nursery was liable to sudden raids. If Grandmama caught us in the act of reading *Comic Cuts* and *Lots o' Fun* she would confiscate them and sail out of the room like a customs ship loaded with contraband, saying "Monsieur Charles Geoffroy-Dechaume* never allows his children to read comic papers." We were left bewildered and forlorn. Who could Monsieur Charles Geoffroy-Dechaume be?

We found her bewildering and exasperating, but we were never frightened of her, and I think that we knew instinctively that she was the genius of the family and that it

---

*A French artist. One of his daughters married my brother Stephen, another my cousin Dermod MacCarthy.

was because of her that everything was of absorbing interest. Nevertheless it was a relief to turn to the accountable 'Gumpaga', always gentle, calm and humorous. As a ritual of salutation we would blow on his gold watch to make it open, and as a farewell we got a very scratchy kiss. His conversation was economical and pointful and he imposed the same high standard as Grandmama in his own way, with an occasional mild reproof.

At the end of the day when staying at Eton we each went up to Gumpaga's study, fresh from a bath, to sit on his lap while he drew a picture with his quill pen, to take to bed. It was a good ending; he could draw beautifully.

Nearly every child of my generation seemed to have at least one maiden aunt. She is now obsolete as a type, but used to be a feature of family life. Those who were talented played the piano or painted in water colours. Others did good works and they often lived in pairs. We had three maiden aunts – one of each kind: Great Aunt Emily, Aunt Margaret, and Aunt Dodo. Great Aunt Emily Ritchie was Grandmama's sister, remarkably different from her, being tall and thin and very self contained. She was an accomplished pianist in spite of her habit of lifting her hands up very high above the keys, so that one wondered how they got back again in time for the next chord. At a concert she would manage to place an exclamation of "charming" most skilfully between the end of a piece of music and the clapping that followed. She and Edith Sichel, an historian, were a devoted pair of spinsters.

In most large Victorian families there was a pre-dominance of girls and the eldest seldom had an honest deal; she was delegated a lot of her parents' responsibilities without being given full authority. This was the fate of Aunt Margaret, the eldest and best looking of the five Cornish sisters; her position in her own home was ambiguous. She painted charming water-colour landscapes and her embroidery was first rate. I was devoted to her as a child as I was her favourite niece.

Stephen was loved passionately by Aunt Dodo who led a life of self-denial rather than touch any of the capital that she meant to bequeath to him. She was a gentle as a dove – an exquisite, frail little person who spoke in a whispering voice that she sometimes raised bravely to a shout. She was very religious and used to give Bible lessons to Stephen and me from an illustrated book. She spoke of someone called Our Saviour and showed us pictures of a square-set man enveloped in a blanket with broad stripes and wearing a heavy head-dress. But the Jesus I adored was called Our Lord – the Jesus of the holy pictures that nuns gave us – dressed in rhubarb pink with long tapering limbs and beautifully combed hair, ending in shoulder length curls. I couldn't accept Aunt Dodo's stocky Our Saviour as the same person, nor could I abide her readings from *Pilgrim's Progress* about people with impossible names, with the blackest engravings as illustrations – I can't read it now. Poor Aunt Dodo, her message didn't get across; her innocence made a better sermon than any amount of Bunyan. She adopted our faith with its sectarian vocabulary after we had grown up, but during our childhood our only co-religionist in the family was Grandmama.

There were three Cornish Uncles: Francis, Hubert, and

Gerald. Uncle Francis had died in India, before I was born, as a gay Cavalry officer and brilliant sportsman. He was a romance to us, and I used to dawdle in passages admiring his drawings where they hung in frames on the walls – illustrations to Rudyard Kipling's *The Jungle Book*, or of hunting scenes; and I loved to read his letters which were published after his death, all about his mares and polo and pig-sticking.

Uncle Hubert lived with his family at Englefield Green, and a long drive in a cab across Windsor Park to stay with him and Aunt Lawrencina, his wife, was a familiar sequel to a visit to The Cloisters. Their eldest son, Francis, was a great friend and I loved staying there. Aunt Lawrencina gave her home a fairy story atmosphere. She was a first rate violinist and the music room was the centre of the family.

The youngest of the three brothers was Gerald, who was our favourite uncle. He was made restless by a romantic idealism, and his progress was eclectic. Having won a double first in the classical tripos he took orders, then relinquished them to go through a phase of neo-paganism, and later became a Christian Scientist. After leaving the church he was appointed lecturer in Greek at Manchester University. At one time he followed Tolstoy's precepts to the extent of giving away his possessions to work as a docker; at another he devoted his spare time to teaching boys in the slums of Manchester to act Greek plays.

At the time of this graecophil phase, he came to stay with us and seemed absorbed by the problem of animating the world through a revival of the Greek way of life. We were a little disappointed at not being able to play the familiar games with him; he was living in another world and wanted to introduce us to it. He made us do Isadora Duncan steps, dancing barefooted on the lawn, chanting as we skipped up and down, and in no time we found ourselves enjoying it. In the evening he made us act a scene from a Greek play, teaching us the strange words with great patience and explaining their meaning with fervour: "Oh children, children hold onto my cloak!" His enthusiasm was infectious.

When war broke out in 1914 he joined the Somerset Light Infantry and usually spent part of his leave staying with us. The badge on his cap included the word Jellalabad (a battle won by his regiment) and we interpreted it as Jerry le Bad, so he wrote a story in the trenches and sent it to us – a delightful fairy story about two kings called Jerry le Bad and Stephen le Good. He was killed in September 1916. Jerry le Bad and Stephen le Good are commemorated on the war memorial at King's College Chapel in Cambridge; both are listed among the scholars, one in each world war.

Next came my mother who combined a strong streak of the family romanticism with practical worldly wisdom; then Aunt Molly MacCarthy, brilliant mimic and brilliant writer, whose delicate and fanciful humour I so much appreciated when I was older but who, to a child, seemed rather distant – wearing an amused and slightly puzzled expression – obviously not much enjoying '*l'oeuvre de mère.*' The youngest was Aunt Cecilia who married into the navy; her husband was William Wordsworth Fisher, later Admiral Sir

William Fisher, popularly known as 'WW'. She was a gay and enjoyable aunt.

I liked my Cornish uncles and aunts one at a time. They were so permeated with the same atmosphere, though extremely individual in character, that I had very much the feeling of being of their own kind. Their sense of humour was piercing but never malicious, and they were all good mimics. Their intellectual vitality was stimulating, and nothing escaped their observation, but to be with several of them together was bewildering.

Conversation was like a tight rope walk – the unforgivable sin was to be 'boring'. Certain subjects such as servants, ailments, or money were absolutely taboo, except 'en tête à tête' – preferably in a bedroom. The problems of the boiler could only be discussed with the boilerman in the boiler-room. They were intolerant of facetiousness, sentimentality, pompousness, pedantry, insincerity, heartiness . . . the list could go on forever: such high standards were discouraging. This extreme fastidiousness made them irritable, but they were far from precious and knew only too well how to criticise themselves. Their conversation would be punctuated with: "Here I am gushing," or "Am I being censorious?" and a lot of chaffing went on between them.

I was embarrassed by the family habit of hurling home truths at each other and I found it hard to understand why Grandmama appeared to enjoy being teased by her children. "Now you're being nice," my mother once said to her, "you were so supercilious a moment ago." Grandmama smiled in silence. They laughed at her openly and were ready to laugh at her with friends so long as those friends appreciated her rare qualities; but they were very sensitive to her being treated as a figure of fun, and angry with anyone who giggled behind her back, as the younger grandchildren were apt to do, or failed to meet her on her own ground.

The mystique about Eton that prevailed at that time was shared whole-heartedly by Grandmama who was much given to mystique, and yet she was not really in her own climate there. What she valued most in human intercourse was the note of authenticity and an original approach to things, and she waged a war of her own against the snobs, the pedants, and the prigs. As to the snobs, she herself was not above a duke – very far from it, thrilled by a duke – but she did not approve of the Eton tradition of looking down on the scholars as poor boys who had to earn their privileges by their wits; she put the intellect above everything and there was a lot that was uncongenial to her. She went about the place with her eyes half closed, shutting them tight when anything dreary came her way, opening them wide to the beauty and historic tradition that surrounded her, and flashing them with red fire at anything inspiring, saying "Intensely interesting". She made the best of what was to hand. There was a constant flow of Etonians from London, some widely cultured neighbours, and there were the wonderful Eton boys, her idols.

She also gathered round her, from far afield, people of her own choice. Of the many famous men she entertained, I can only remember G.K. Chesterton. He came to a luncheon party – so large that it was given in the Audit Room. Our cousin Peggy Ritchie was then staying at

The Cloisters, and she and David and I were allowed to attend it as a special privilege. We were told beforehand who was going to be there, and given a list of celebrated names. Mr so-and-so was a "most delightful person" and Professor so-and-so "tremendously distinguished". I didn't take much of it in, but I do remember looking down on Chesterton as he came up the stairs from the hall, and noticing the pile of dark red curls on his head. My mother greeted him on the landing and introduced me to him, and then I could only see his thick woollen stockings and a large expanse of tweed knickerbockers; but I felt attracted to him and liked his genial voice and the rich laugh that came rumbling up from the depths of him, though I could hardly see his face.

When they were all assembled, Grandmama led her collection of literary lions along the Gallery to the Audit Room – an impressive procession, with Peggy, David and me following behind.

That luncheon party was the greatest pleasure to me. Peggy was a good deal older than us and I hero-worshipped her. She sat with David and me at a small table in one of the windows, and we carried on what seemed to me brilliant adult conversation as we ate a delicious meal ending with raspberries and whipped cream.

The great gentlemen sat at a long refectory table in the middle of the room with Grandmama at the head of it, and when they were having their coffee, Chesterton turned round to look at us for a long time with appreciation; he was a great child lover. Mrs Chesterton once told me how annoyed a hostess had been when, having got him to her table with St John Irvine, he had deliberately kept the conversation on children for most of the evening. Speaking as one famous man to another he had asked "Do you like babies?" St John Irvine had replied: "Oh yes! especially at the comet stage," meaning in the long white clothes in which infants were then dressed.

Chesterton was not a frequent guest. The two constant habitués were Donald Tovey and Maurice Baring.

Donald Tovey was a musical genius, a concert pianist and music critic and a composer. The son of an Eton master, he had gravitated as a little boy towards the Cornish nursery as to his own habitat, and had taken his place there as one more brother, continuing as a frequent inmate of The Cloisters until the Cornish children had all left home. He became Professor of Music at Edinburgh University in 1914; his musical criticism is still remembered and quoted. As I remember him, he seemed to be wholly absorbed in music. He hummed when not talking and liked to talk sitting at the piano, using it as a second voice as he illustrated jokes and anecdotes about famous composers, or improvised settings to comic verse. After a while he would become more serious and, detaching himself from his hearers, drift irresistibly into the brilliant performance of some classical piece.

His remarkable talents were spotted and nurtured from childhood by Miss Weisse, a German woman of forceful personality, who first ran an infants' school at Eton and later started a boarding-school, called Northlands, for the sisters of Eton boys. My mother and her younger sisters attended both these schools, and so did Donald Tovey.

Miss Weisse, with her German connections, had every means of providing him with a first rate musical education. The concerts at Northlands were outstanding with Donald always at the piano.

Maurice Baring had also begun to frequent the family in early youth, as a schoolboy. Over the years he built up an intimate friendship with each of the Cornishes, particularly with my grandmother, with whom he kept up a continuous correspondence. I remember his restless impatience when a conversation was interrupted, and how he would rush to the bookshelves, putting a monocle into his eye, and take out one book after the other with his trembling hands – already in his youth a slow creeping paralysis had begun to affect him.

He was one of a large family and initiated all his closer friends to the language and lore of his own childhood. We and our cousins were all brought up on the Baring vocabulary, with expressions such as 'Arch Baker' for a long and boring discourse, 'Aunt Sister' for the shirking of a social duty, 'padlock' – a private confidence, and so on. He always called my mother Scarlet, and when he took to typing his letters because of his trembling hands, he went to the trouble of changing to the red tape to print her name.

At Cambridge the rooms that my father shared with Gerald Warre Cornish were in the Gibbs building at King's, right opposite the porter's lodge. When Maurice visited them, he couldn't bear to waste time by going round the quad, so he used to throw his gown over his head and take a forbidden path across the grass on all fours, pretending to be a quadruped. This childish playfulness and love of practical jokes persisted in him into his old age. Though not a rich man, he was lavishly generous and fond of giving presents. When my parents were in South Africa, he had mounted for them in the most luxurious binding a single line from Virgil printed on one page: *'Tendebant que manusripae ulterioris amore'* – a book of five words. 'They stretch out their hands with longing to be the first to cross over.'

I was once the only child present when three London hostesses were assembled together at The Cloisters – Mrs Saxton Noble (Celia), in an enormous hat under which many kisses were skilfully manoeuvred, Mrs Leigh Smith, with a hint of a French accent, who was very tall and impressively dignified, and Mrs Hammersley, unusually short. They were all three dressed in great style, each with individuality. I should have been overawed had not Mrs Leigh Smith sat on a chair to bring herself to my level and drawn me to her to say that if she had a little girl, she would wish her to be just like me. This set me at my ease.

Like so many girls I had longed to be a boy from my earliest years and I thought to be an Eton boy must be the most wonderful experience possible. I wished that I could have a top hat to stroke against my sleeve as they did, and I thought that their sports clothes were too beautiful for words. Though I couldn't see the boy who was shouting, I felt that I would have given anything to be able to answer his call of "Boy! Boy!" and to do any kind of menial task for him.

At the beginning of the century, the cult of male youth

was prevalent, and the chaste sportsman was the ideal. The Englishwoman was rather left in the lurch and not quite sure of her ground. I hadn't a clue as to what I was expected to grow up into, but I vowed secretly that I would never be like the ladies of Eton. So many of them gave me a vague impression of unhappiness. A contemporary American lady said "In England nothing is for women – not even the men." Of Eton it could have been said then: "especially not the men". The public school attitude towards a woman was of someone almost superfluous and rather indecent. I don't believe that French girls were ever made to feel so rejected.

When we had outgrown the nursery, Hester and I had many restrictions imposed on us as granddaughters of the Vice-Provost, and they humiliated me. We weren't supposed to go into the town without wearing our best hats and gloves, and if we met a boy we knew it was better not to recognise him. On Sundays no sort of pastime was allowed where we might be seen.

My memories of Eton are mostly pre-1914 when the fashions were rather nondescript. The leg of mutton sleeve was out and the hobble skirt was not yet in. The ideal female figure of the period was inhumanly round with an enormous undivided bust like a football, and a tiny waist that flowed with an *art nouveau* swoop into a second football below.

The long skirt was often draped by an overskirt falling to what seemed to me just the wrong length. The top was generally a cross-over bodice covered with fussy accessories, sometimes with a high-necked slip underneath. A square flat muff was held low and limply, and an enormous straight hat was pinned perilously onto a high coiffure. The whole get up needed the right sort of deportment to carry it off – if not it became extraordinarily dowdy. I once saw a lady wearing a dress that had two rows of buttons behind, below the waist, as though to emphasise the fact that the lower balloon consisted of two buttocks, and I was scandalised. Buttoned boots which were considered so elegant, revolted me. They went up high enough to touch the long petticoats, and the mixture of black leather and white lace seemed to me nightmarish – the feather boa gave me the same thrill of horror. I was acutely aware of the ugliness of these clothes and their incongruity on the chaste bodies of my aunts. Few English ladies could bring themselves to show them to advantage. Yvette Guilbert used to sing a song about them:

> "Les Misses pudiques
> 'J'ai le derrière britannique
> Defendu – n'y touchez pas!' "

My Aunts all had the habit of dipping their heads as though the huge hats were too heavy for their necks. But fashion required that the chin should be held up, the bust thrust forward proudly, and the thighs shown to advantage – a naughty, provocative sort of deportment. I didn't like it when it was correct and I had the uncomfortable feeling of something being wrong when it wasn't.

Dress was a great problem for my mother and her sisters. It was thought vulgar – almost immoral – in their circle to be too fashionable, and yet they wanted to achieve what they called distinction. It was frivolous to give too much time or money to clothes (not that they had much to spend) yet unforgivable to be dowdy, and they liked to be original without being arty. My mother tended to wear clothes that were too grand for the occasion – perhaps a fault on the right side. She had great dignity of presence and, unknown to her, Uncle Desmond called her the 'Contessa'.

I remember Aunt Margaret coming up to me at a cricket match to say "Of course I realise that my dress is much too young for me. I must look ridiculous." At Rachel's wedding, Aunt Molly said to me aside "I hate my dress . . . bride's mother . . . wine red." It was in fact a charming and becoming dress. My Grandmother had no such problems. Like all old ladies she wore clothes that were out of fashion in her own perennial style.

On one visit to Eton, when we were an extra large party of cousins – Balfours and MacCarthys, three of each – we got quite out of control, as this little episode will show.

In summer, flower-boxes were brought out onto the leads to make a roof garden. One evening a gardener's boy came to arrange the flowers and when Grandmama was called away he performed a feat of daring to show off to us. There was another building with a flat roof opposite the leads and a brick arch framing a door between the two buildings. The intrepid boy crossed over this arch to the other side by the single course of bricks and came back just in time, giving me a wink as Grandmama reappeared.

The next morning I took Michael onto the leads and persuaded him to cross onto the arch. He was younger than me but I made him go first. As I was standing spell-bound watching his careful progress, there was a sudden shriek from the schoolroom window. We had been seen! I was summoned to face a row of formidable females – two aunts and my grandmother who said "You know Clare, Grandmama nearly fainted." The elders then withdrew to the dining room for a *conseil de famille*, and agitated voices could be heard through the door. When at last they subsided a new rule of discipline was instantly enforced. We were separated and each set to a different task. Mine was 'The Lady of Shalott', which I tried to learn by heart as I sat on the wooden steps of the leads looking appropriately towards Windsor Castle and the 'tirra-lirra' river.

This was before the days of the telephone, yet a governess called Miss Elphick was found at once with the greatest efficiency. She descended on us like an avenging angel. "You don't know it very well, do you?" she said, trying to make her kind face look stern, when I had stammered through the first two verses of Tennyson's poem.

Presently a procession was led solemnly down the Gallery to the Audit Room: Grandmother, Aunt, Governess, Hester and me, with little Rachel MacCarthy trotting beside us chattering away with a doll in her arms.

As a last and glorious act of vandalism, I pulled back the governess's chair just as she was about to sit down – and with perfect success – her fat bottom nearly touched the ground; but she spoilt the fun by pretending to be amused, and our lessons began as if nothing had happened. They were excellent lessons. Grace Elphick was to teach us in London and to become a great friend. She later became a contemplative nun and Mother Superior of a Carmelite Convent.

In the meantime, Stephen and Michael were marched off to the dining-room for a reading lesson, but teaching was not one of Aunt Molly's many talents – she was the last person to fix a child's attention, her own mind being full of imaginative fantasy. The boy's lessons ended as ours had begun – with an act of rebellion; Michael, spelling aloud from *Reading without Tears* read "C-A-T – Kitten", and threw the book into the corner of the room. Reading that morning was not without tears. Aunt Margaret, experienced from having taught her younger sisters their first lessons, took the boys for their reading the following days and imposed stable government.

It was at about this time that Mrs Hammersley kept a gondola at her house at Bourne End. How enchanted my grandmother would have been had she been rowed to Fellows' Eyot by her Italian gondolier! But she always went to Eton from Windsor station by cab. Grandmama and Mrs Hammersley were the greatest friends although of different generations, and they both had the same piercing black eyes. When they met, they used to advance towards each other with the same prolonged "Ah . . . !" in unison, as a greeting.

I have a vivid recollection of the welcome that Grandmama gave to the Bishop who came to consecrate the newly built chapel for Catholic Eton boys. The Prince of the Church was standing at the door – a very handsome man, resplendent in heliotrope. She advanced towards him with brisk little steps and managed a curtsey, the kissing of his ring, and a very eloquent "Ah . . . !" in perfect co-ordination. Later as she and Mrs Hammersley sat together waiting for the ceremony to begin, she leant towards her and whispered loudly "Kind Lord Grey! [the donor of the chapel] Fascinating Bishop! Isn't it fascinating to look at that Bishop and to know that he will never have a wife?"

Before this chapel was built Sunday church-going used to take up the whole morning. We walked along the High Street with straggling Catholic Eton boys, Grandmama slowing down our pace, and up the steep hill to Windsor, sometimes crossing the river by ferry. After a long sung mass with a sermon, we would go and visit the parish priest, Canon Longenotto, as he ate his breakfast stroking a large white cat. (Grandmama pronounced his name with a perfect Italian accent); then slowly home again on foot. A cab was only hired in wet weather.

The school authorities altered the boundary soon after the chapel was built, making it out of bounds, so the Catholic Eton boys once again had to obtain permission to go to it.

When we stayed with our grandparents, most of the people who came to the house were special family friends, but there were occasional uncongenial visitors, and sometimes it seemed as if Grandmama were charged with electricity and letting off sparks – a row with a master was not uncommon. When one of these masters wrote to apologise for a quarrel he had had with her, he ended his letter by saying "I am in the world but not of it". She read this last sentence aloud at the breakfast table and added "But so many people I know are of the world but not in it".

Like most people with strong feelings she was given to outbursts of anger. I never resented these because they were spontaneous and straight-forward and quickly over. They were not frequent; but I will give an example.

A lady, whom I will call Mrs Jenkins, just had to be invited. She was a kind-hearted lady but she was silly, and Grandmama abhorred silliness. As we sat waiting for her round the tea table at the open French window, Aunt Margaret was in the middle of irritating Grandmama, when Mrs Jenkins was announced. She waddled into the room beaming in flounces of rustling taffeta.

Gumpaga, at the beginning of his last illness, was sitting in his wheel chair – the silver hair on his temples even longer than usual, and he looked a perfectly sweet old man; but Mrs Jenkins shouldn't have said that he did, nor should she have leant forward so often to stroke the sleeve of his velvet jacket and croon over him.

By the time that we had finished our tea, Grandmama was pacing up and down in front of the door at the back of the room, like a wild animal in a cage, and when Mrs Jenkins at last took her leave, she made the fatal mistake of giving Gumpaga a kiss with a resounding smack. An ominous imperative came from the other end of the room: "Come here, Mrs Jenkins". Mrs Jenkins obeyed, making towards the door with her hand innocently outstretched to say goodbye. Then we heard three more resounding smacks, of a different kind from the first, to Grandmama's "There, there, there!"

A short silence followed, and then a wail like that of a child of five was slowly raised; Gumpaga chuckled, and

Aunt Margaret jumped up to take Mrs Jenkins out into the garden and console her. The wailing went on there, and was so loud that the Lytteltons, thinking that a child had been hurt, looked out of the window, and were very surprised to see what they saw.

Neither Stephen nor I had dared to look round to see what was happening at the other end of the room. We had never known grown-ups to behave like that before. To our surprise the scene was recalled by the family with laughter for several days after. Everyone was agreed that Mrs Jenkins had had her deserts, and Grandmama smiled silently.

On the whole I was less disconcerted by this sort of behaviour than by the way that Grandmama had of showering her praises in some unexpected quarter – when a phrase such as the 'farmer poet', or 'Juliet's nurse', would flash into her mind and give some quite uninteresting person an aura. I used to watch people getting a kind of vertigo from being placed on her pedestal, then slowly regaining their balance at the unaccustomed height.

Eton society had never had anyone quite like Grandmama before – not anyone who might invite some guests to tea and then decide that it would be better if they all read books instead of talking; who would ask at a dinner party "What's the time, Frank? It feels like midnight." Or shut her eyes in a crowded room and be heard to murmur: "Yes, she always wore purple in Lent."

When she was dying and was told who had presented her with a magnificent bouquet of flowers she said: "A millionaire – how boring!" These are reputed to have been her last words.

She made a fable of the name Warre Cornish, and it was not until my grandfather's third successor moved into the Vice-Provost's house that the brass plate bearing his name was removed from the front door.

Eton was permeated with the fairy-land atmosphere of the Edwardian age. Looking back I see it in perfect summer weather. As we play with our cousins, the grown-ups are in the background having their own fun, walking on stretches of the smoothest grass under elegant parasols, or gliding on the river in punts, laughing often as they talk in intimacy with their cultured friends.

Everything was expected to be exquisite, and everything generally was.

ETON

The Cloisters

ALTHOUGH my mother came sixth in her family she was the first to marry, so our grandparents took great interest in us, their first grandchildren, and we spent a lot of our childhood at Eton, paying them long visits at different times of the year.

Their house was one of four, known then as The Cloisters, that are relegated to the four College Fellows: Provost, Headmaster, Bursar, and Vice Provost – a Jacobean terrace flanking two sides of the mediaeval cloister. Above the cloister is a wide gallery into which each of the Fellows' houses leads. The third side incorporates the College Hall with the Library above it, and the fourth has an arch under the clock leading into the schoolyard where the statue of the founder, Henry VI, stands surrounded by buildings of

1. Mr Warre Cornish,
   Vice-Provost of Eton

2. Mrs Warre Cornish
   with Hester and David

3. Reggie and Charlotte Balfour

5. Clare

4. Mrs Warre Cornish

6. Aunt Molly (Later Mrs Desmond McCarthy)

7. Tea in the garden at Ford

8. Hilaire Belloc on the *Nona*

9. David

10. Clare

11. Stephen

12. Hester

blood-red brick and the slender grey chapel. The windows of the Fellows' houses overlook their communal garden and the meadow beyond it, Fellows' Eyot, along which the Thames flows. The Vice Provost's house, being on a corner, also commands a view of Windsor Castle towering above willow trees.

The school clock struck very loud in its tower and, though we never knew the time of day, it gave a rhythm to our lives and a sense of the life of the school going on apart from ours – as did the sound of cricket bats that could be heard from the garden in summer.

The rooms were decorated in the William Morris style with marquetry furniture and Delft china on shelves. William Morris tapestries and chintzes draped every window and piece of upholstery; birds and plants were the ever repeated theme of decoration, blue and green the predominant colours. Medici prints hung on William Morris wallpapers with many of Mrs Cameron's photographs. Here and there a William de Morgan plate or a Della Robbia plaque was placed over a door; a dark blue and green tapestry, representing a classical scene, hung at one end of the long drawing-room.

There were five doors to the house which gave it a sense of impending surprise, and the people coming in from them seemed to come each from a different world. Three were on the ground floor. The official front door was in the cloister leading into a dark and gloomy hall. It was much less used by the family than a back door, near the tradesman's entrance, that was approached from a quiet lane and through a walled garden. On the upper floor there was another door from the gallery and one from the garden, up a flight of iron steps. They gave a sense of freedom to the house.

From an early age I enjoyed the beauty of Eton and nowhere else was I so aware of the summer. I loved to hear the sound of water lapping against the side of a punt and the echo of the cloister, to feel the throb of hot weather coming into the house with the throb of the mowing machine bringing the smell of cut grass through large open windows, and I delighted in the profusion of flowers from the Fellows' communal garden, of which Grandmama always had more than her fair share. She used to send me to the head gardener with her order for fear of being rebuffed by him, and I resented the way he scolded me for her greed. "Mrs Cornish has all the flowers. There are never any left for Mrs Lyttelton."*

I can remember walking from the walled garden to the house, my arms laden with flowers, alternately burying my nose in a moss rose and sniffing at a lily of the valley, trying to decide which gave me most delight. Grandmama had asked which was my favourite flower, and I felt that I had to decide.

In summer we spent a lot of time in the part of Fellows' Eyot that turns round by a backwater where the kingfishers darted across the brown stream – a corner of the meadow that seemed to be the favourite grazing of the old and bronchial sheep. It was here that we fished under red may trees to the roar of the weir, and watched cygnets riding on

*Mrs Lyttelton, wife of the headmaster, Edward Lyttelton.

their parents' backs. The sight of Mr Luxmore was a further enhancement as he went to and from the little bridge that led to his island garden – a beautiful old man with flowing white hair and an aquiline profile.

In fine weather the centre of family life was 'the leads', a flat roof onto which the drawing-room opened to the side. Here Grandmama would sit for hours writing her letters with a squeaky quill pen, her feet on a footstool and a board on her knees. The squeak was erratic, with long interruptions while she gazed abstractedly at her surroundings or shut her eyes, as was her habit. She had a way of speaking her thoughts aloud, and was heard to say during one of these pauses "Kipps, not Kipling. Kim, not Joachim." Then the pen would resume its squeaking as she went on with her letter.

In the evening when the last post was heard from the castle barracks, she would take me by the hand and lead me imperatively onto the leads, ordering me to look up to Windsor and be inspired by the sound that came floating over the valley – and so I always was.

At Christmas she used to give large children's parties in the College Hall, preceded by carol singing by candlelight before a crib that she arranged in a cellar off the cloister. This was something quite unknown in those days and rather smacked of popery, but she called it a 'crêche', and that gave it an acceptable label. When we had sung our carols, we went up the wide stone staircase to the hall where enormous logs burned in the two fireplaces, and there was a large Christmas tree. After tea we played games and more carols were sung by choristers.

Gumpaga did his reading and writing upstairs in his study, which led to the turret room where he slept. Grandmama used to stand at the foot of the stairs and call up to him "Frank! Frank!" and when he did join the family it was rather as an onlooker, standing with his hands on the lapels of his coat, or sitting apart with his legs crossed limply, twitching his free foot (a habit inherited by at least two of his grandsons) and chuckling at the conversation. In winter he liked to stand with his back to the fire, warming his hands behind him, and I used to wait anxiously for the backward kick that he gave from time to time to the logs without turning round to look at them – so quickly that his spats hadn't time to catch fire.

We slept with Nana at the top of the house in an attic room with a turret room beyond it, and there was another little room known as 'The Slit' that was generally given to a nursery maid. The William Morris wallpapers and chintzes spread like creepers up to the top floor and all over these rooms.

Our visits often overlapped or coincided with our younger cousins, especially Michael and Rachel MacCarthy who were nearest in age. When Stephen and I were in bed Uncle Desmond, their father, used sometimes to come up and tell us stories. He told them better than anyone else, but he had the idea that fear made children imaginative, and deliberately chose ghost stories and thrillers. Then we were left in the haunted attics with our imaginations beautifully stimulated, while the nurses and grown-ups went down to an inaccessible part of the house for their evening meal. He was the most kind and sympathetic man and we enjoyed his company, as he clearly enjoyed ours, but he liked to spice his relationship with us with a little tinge of fear.

In the day-time we crowded into a tiny room next to the dining-room called the schoolroom. It was much too small for large parties of children, but I don't think we ever felt cramped there. I can remember Hester and David in that little room, absorbed in adding to their stamp collection by cutting early Victorian stamps from the pile of old envelopes that Grandmama had given them, shouting with excitement when they found them unperforated or, better still, a farthing stamp; and Rachel (aged four) declaring her love for Stephen (aged eight), sitting on the arm of his chair and saying "Let me kiss your dear hair again." It was a touching scene, but I could never have shown my affection for Stephen with Rachel's spontaneity, and I was glad when David put an end to it by jeering at her.

As the dining-room door opened and shut at meals we heard the roar of grown-up conversation, and we were allowed in at the end of lunch – only privileged to eat with the family one at a time, in turn.

The dining-room at The Cloisters, though it had a sideboard, a big round table, and a set of twelve chairs covered with frilled Morris chintzes, had none of the formal atmosphere of most dining-rooms. In each of the windows on either side of the fireplace there was a French armchair covered in rust-coloured velvet, and Grand-mama's writing desk – marquetry of course and covered with birds and flowers – stood against a wall. Portraits of the Warre family, wigged, and faintly smiling, hung on all the walls: a Hogarth, Romney and a Kneller. I didn't like the look of those ancestors and had a loathing of six little people in oval frames, three over each of the doors, with rosy cheeks and shiny lips – the ladies most disgracefully *décolleté*.

We were allowed in and out of the dining-room freely, and here practical every day things could be discussed – the drawing-room set a higher standard of conversation. My grandparents had the habit of leaving the table before the meal was over to sit in one of the armchairs, joining in the conversation from a distance. At one Sunday tea party, throughout which Grandmama sat at the window with her eyes shut, she made only one remark: "I dislike the sound of church bells on Sunday – so Hanoverian!"

The word 'elevenses' had not yet been coined, but the habit of a mid-morning collation was indulged in by the Warre Cornishes half a century before it was given a name, and was taken out of a large breakfast cup of the pattern known as Blue Danish. Here Aunt Dodo would be found at 10.45 drinking Benger's Food as she – a pious maiden lady – waited for a fly to take her to work in the slums of Hackney Wick, and Grandmama would pause in her writing to have what she called *café au lait*.

One morning I was surprised to find Gumpaga there in court dress taking some light refreshment before going to a levee at St James's, and Grandmama explained to me the meaning of the word and described the French kings' levees. Gumpaga looked tiny and elegant in his black breeches and silk stockings, and far from giving the impression of fancy dress, seemed more like himself than in the tail coat that he usually wore.

Another contact with the monarch was an occasional haunch of venison when a stag was sent from Windsor Park for the Fellows, but I didn't like the taste of venison; indeed, the dining-room food was full of dangers. Grandmama was inclined to introduce a French touch and you never knew what sort of surprise a sauce might bring. I was once made miserable for a whole afternoon by tasting a piece of Camembert, and when I ate a liqueur chocolate by mistake I felt as if a cruel joke had been played on me. The venison was royal and could be spoken of, but Grandmama didn't like too much talk about food at table. At one dinner party when the menu was being discussed, she suddenly said "And then the fox – how delicious!"

One early morning I opened the dining-room door and barged in on family prayers. Gumpaga was sitting and reading from a bible, and a collection of servants were kneeling on the floor in pale cotton frocks and white aprons and caps. Aunt Dodo, who gave me a sidelong glance of disapproval, was the only one of the family there. I thought that it was a very funny affair – they seemed to pray in a different way from us, and I must have behaved flippantly because I was told never to attend again.

This is the only time that I remember seeing all the servants; there must have been quite a number of them for such a large household, but the only one I can give a name to was Janet. She wore an extra large cap on top of her head like a white blancmange. We sometimes went into the kitchen to fetch the parrot, which we were allowed to carry out into the garden in its cage, but I have no recollection of a cook. Apart from Janet I only remember the boot boy; he worked in a little room near the back door where I watched him sticking knives into slits in a wooden drum, then turning a handle round to clean them with a crunching noise.

The gardeners were great friends: Saunders, the young head gardener, old Marsh with a wispy white beard, Ambrose, and the flat-footed Albert. Marsh had once proposed to Miss Crabbe, the dressmaker, shouting at her through the kitchen window, and had been instantly refused. This was a story that she would tell time and time again like a favourite tune, with the refrain "And he popped a little bunch of flowers on the window sill."

I seldom understood what the grown-ups were talking about at Eton. Aunt Margaret once asked me to fetch a pack of cards from the marquetry chest next to the powder magazine in the lobby. It was like being spoken to in a foreign language, but there was one clue: the word lobby was familiar. On the landing leading to the gallery was a little room known as the lobby pantry that was used as a flower room, but I had always thought that the word was an adjective. The pantry was nice and very lobby – you could make a lot of mess there – and now the word had disconcertingly turned into a noun. Not wanting to betray my ignorance, I went off in search of the cards. I didn't know how hot I was as I stood in the lobby itself, just beside the drawer that contained them, baffled by those extraordinary words: Marquetry, I thought, must have something to do with a market, and powder magazine? . . . David read the Sherlock Holmes stories from the *Strand Magazine*. Was there some connection between them? As I found no solution to these riddles, I went back to Aunt Margaret empty handed, and she was much irritated at my inefficiency.

There were so many mysteries at Eton. The powder magazine, as I learnt later, was the Dutch cabinet in which, amongst other things, the key of the library was kept, but why was it so called? Why not Fellows' Four since there were four Fellows? And why Audit Room? Was there a verb 'to aud'? And how was it that Aunt Dodo was High Church, Aunt Margaret Low Church, and Gumpaga Broad Church, when they all worshipped in the same chapel? It didn't occur to me that these questions might be given satisfactory answers, so I went on wondering.

We often played in the gallery above the cloister with its

blue carpet and its walls covered with framed portraits. It was just not too frightening to be enjoyable. Each of the Fellows' houses had a door opening out onto it, and we took off our shoes to run about on the blue felt in fear of being heard. The Bursar, Mr Galthrop, frequently burst out of his, and though we knew him well, as he was a next door neighbour, we never quite got used to his blindness. He once surprised Stephen and me as we played and said "I can't see you but I can feel you," and he crouched down waving his arms about in Blind Man's Buff movements. He caught hold of Stephen and flung him over his shoulder to smack him playfully. Hester slowed down our hazardous progress by making a rule that every crowned portrait should be honoured with a curtsey or a bow. She enjoyed the feminine gesture.

After the Bursar's the next door to get past was the Headmaster's. We often went into his house by the door near the mulberry tree in the garden, when his daughters Nora and Delia gave us a lovely welcome. He had the slowest laugh – so slow that I used to wonder if he was really laughing – and this put me off him. We felt quite at our ease in his house, but somehow the Gallery door was different to the garden door, and behind it he became the abstract headmaster, so we quickened our pace as we ran past it lest the Great Panjandrum himself should pounce upon us, birch-rod in hand, like the headmaster of the Caldecot picture book.

Once past that door the worst was over. The Audit Room was nearly always empty, then came the Provost's door and that was 'home'. Edmund Warre, who was then Provost,

was my grandfather's cousin (old and infirm by the time that I knew him) and his daughter Joan adored us and spoilt us with crackers and sweets. We were glad when that door opened.

The Library we felt was part of our home. My grandfather, being librarian, spent a lot of time there and allowed us in. At the far end of it there was a model of the College in a glass case which we loved to look at, and in a corner near it there was a spiral staircase leading up to the turret room. This little room was filled with enormous books in leather bindings, faded and peeling, and the floor was littered with large dead moths. We imagined that a little old man went there when nobody was about and sat cross-legged on the floor to read the huge books.

One day, coming in from a walk, I went into the library to see Gumpaga and made straight for the model of Eton. When he had finished his work, he called me and as he didn't hear me answer, he thought that I must have gone out without his noticing me, and he left the library, locking the door behind him. There followed for me what seemed like hours of agony. If I shouted for help, the little old man in the turret room would hear me. I didn't dare to call out but I couldn't help crying. Then at last I was heard by Aunt Molly and was released. When Uncle Desmond heard of my adventure, he came in to the schoolroom and took me on his knee to whisper in my ear, several times, as I refused to answer "Did you cry?" Of course I had cried, and of course everybody knew that I had. Why should he tease me about it?

The next time that he played with us, he took Stephen and me, to Nana's great disapproval, all over the roof, climbing out from the nursery window and walking along the leads to where we could look down onto the schoolyard. Then we went down a dark spiral staircase and shouted for Mr Wright the porter, who unlocked the door. To our great surprise we stepped out into the cloister. This expedition made up for all his teasing.

I have already spoken of Mr Luxmore. His house in the lane leading to the town was also covered all over in green, a style of decoration that the intelligentsia had adopted as a kind of national flag.

One of our social duties was 'boys' breakfasts'. A selection from the school were invited at intervals, and Hester and

I sometimes had to help Grandmama entertain them. Dressed in our party clothes, we were made to force second helpings on the poor guests, too shy to refuse, and were expected to keep the conversation flowing, however tongue tied they might be.

Speaking of Grandmama, A.C. Benson the novelist described his own embarrassment: "She suddenly asked me, before two schoolfellows, through whose eyes I looked on nature? I was dumb, and seeing my consternation, she prompted me by adding, after an awe-inspiring pause, 'Through Kingsley's . . . ?' She was considered to be formidabler by the boys because she asked such disconcerting questions."

As for Hester and me, we were thankful if we got through the meal without her saying anything more startling than "Have some marmalade – so tonic!"

We didn't know how many friendships were made at these breakfasts with some of the boys – friendships that sometimes lasted till the end of her life.

WITTERSHAM

The Balfours

AFTER the eccentricity of the Cornishes it was a relief to be supported by the conventional background of our Balfour grandparents, who gathered a large family round them in the summer months at Wittersham in Kent.

Wittersham House had belonged to my father's brother-in-law Alfred Lyttelton. Alfred died young, and his impoverished widow, Aunt DD, was happy to let her parents take over the running of the house. Originally the village rectory, it had been enlarged by Edwin Lutyens into a spacious four-sided building with wide passages and many French windows leading into the garden – all built round a small and rather dismal courtyard.

My memories of Wittersham are mostly September memories: chestnuts breaking open as they dropped onto the ground; Mary Lyttelton, baroque in her underclothes, leaning from an *oeil de boeuf* to pinch the ripening figs on the wall; or chasing wasps round the dining-room with her table napkin; oil lamps being brought into the drawing-room by the puffing butler Downes as we lingered at the tea table; and the nauseating smell of hops.

The whole of Wittersham was white. The old timbered cottages in the village with palings to their front gardens were painted white. So were the posts of the gate to the house with chains hanging between them, and so was the house itself, inside and out.

We climbed up and down the bars of white gates and went through a white wicket gate in a heavy-scented box hedge, with hot pennies held tight in our hands, to a tiny village shop. The bell made a loud 'ping' as the door opened, and on a shelf was a row of little jars containing red, yellow, and green acid drops in the shape of shells and fish at a penny each; but if you bought sweets loose in a paper bag, the pennyworth was larger.

As at Eton the night nursery was an attic room, but a much larger one and even more frightening because it had been turned into a theatre and had a stage at the far end. It was the greatest fun in the day time to play with the stage properties that had been left behind, but at night it was terrifying.

A Japanese screen standing in one corner had a snarling Samurai warrior painted on each panel, and with a change of temperature the strings of a musical instrument would now and then give off a twang.

Stephen woke up screaming one night and told me of a nightmare he had had about giant cats, and they became another terror to join the many others behind the stage curtain. The stage had been set up by Aunt DD, who had a great interest in the theatre and had collaborated with Miss Lilian Baylis in the early days of the Old Vic. DD was a member of the National Theatre Committee of which her husband Alfred was chairman (the Lyttelton Theatre on the South Bank is named after them).

We never acted on the Wittersham stage, but Hester and David were once enlisted by Aunt DD for a charity performance at the Royal Court Theatre (Stephen and I were too little) to join a chorus of curly-headed angels in the production of a play about St Ursula. Mrs Patrick Campbell took the leading part and Lady Cynthia Asquith that of St Ursula, in spite of a hectic telegram from abroad from her father: 'Forbid you appear on stage in bed'. Nana stood with them in the wings with a team of other nannies, wrapping and unwrapping their angelic charges in shawls, as they made their entries and exits, winged and as nearly naked as the prevailing conventions allowed.

I thought that Granny Balfour was perfect. She was a tiny little lady and an invalid with a bad leg. She would sometimes walk about with a stick, but I remember her chiefly sitting in a chair, never eating meals with the family and never occupied. Early in the evening two footmen came to carry her upstairs in a chair on shafts. She was covered with a mass of pearls and sapphires, had silver white hair and a voice like a silver bell. She was completely feminine – gentle and affectionate though determined, and probably quite uninteresting. Her diction was old fashioned. She said "don't 'ee know" and "ain't it?"

We used to visit her every morning in her bedroom and play with a carriage clock that she kept by her bed; it had a button on it that made it chime when pressed, so that she could tell the time in the night without having to strike a match. When she had a serious illness in London the street was strewn with straw in front of the house, as was often done in the days of carriages to deaden the sound of clopping hooves. I was overwhelmed with pity for Granny when I saw that thick straw stretching as far as I could see. I thought how terribly ill she must have been – the illest person in the world.

Bumpa, as we called our grandfather, would hover round her, solicitous and *desoeuvré* – a fine figure of an old man

with a grey beard, but age didn't suit him. He had few intellectual interests and little life outside his family. With us, he was affectionate and kind but quite out of touch. When he saw us he would say "Well, how many cubic feet have you added to your stature?" and after a meal "Have you filled up your bread basket?" He maintained at breakfast that the true Scotsman should speak of porridge in the plural and he made a point of eating them standing, and that was Scottish too. It is sad that children so seldom have anything to learn from their grandfathers.

My father's brothers and sisters had all married, so that uncles and aunts abounded at Wittersham, and sometimes outnumbered the children. They all had big white handsome faces; they were all forthcoming, straight-forward, affectionate and energetic – to a child all rather the same sort of person. Aunt DD and Aunt May were full of gaiety and enthusiasm. I admired Aunt May's well-proportioned athletic figure and strong hand-made shoes, and I thought that it was dashing of her to play golf. Think of a Cornish aunt doing that!

The uncles were always ready to talk to one, to chat and to play – Uncle Montie, Uncle Duggie and Uncle Tom. What was there to choose between them? Their company was always enjoyable.

Uncle Montie (Arthur Montague) told us his name was "Our Thermometer Balfour." There was a childish irrespon-sibility about him which was a delight to us. He had a streak of vulgarity, and we enjoyed his rude jokes and the music-hall songs that he sang as he went about with us:

> "I want to go home and see that little girl of mine
> and to cuddle up, cuddle up
> That would suit me fine."

or

> "Some o' the time I fancy a brunette
> Sorter one that's got a Spanish mother."

After being impoverished by the Russian Revolution he had dreams of making a second fortune through various ventures in the city, conceiving vast projects like an Ibsen character; but from these his Russian wife, Valerie, wisely dissuaded him. "Morntee," she would say, "he has no idea, he has no idea."

There were generally cousins staying at Wittersham. Oliver Lyttelton was a grand Eton boy who looked down his nose at us kids, and I never dared to say a word to him; but his sister Mary, although several years older than Hester, was always our equal, and we were flattered by her friendship. Then there were the four Talbots with whom we enjoyed ourselves wildly, and Uncle Tom's three daughters collectively known as 'the Troika', younger than us but nevertheless our friends, and sometimes Cecilia Balfour whose father, Uncle Christopher, had died.

Life at Wittersham consisted very largely of games – diabolo, croquet, bowls and tennis which the uncles were very willing to teach us. (The lawns were kept smooth by a little pony with leather boots laced up over its hooves that was led up and down by a gardener as it dragged a wide mowing machine behind it.) Chess and draughts and cards were brought out in the evening, and if there was reading aloud, the books were to our taste, such as *Jock of the Bushveld* and Rudyard Kipling.

All this we vastly preferred to the intellectual readings at Eton and yet it was not so much our climate. For one thing our religion could hardly be tolerated – there wasn't even a sense of strained broadmindedness as with the Cornishes, nor the admission that some things were all right for some people, and I had the impression that everything to do with the Catholic Church sent cold shivers down Balfour spines.

Somebody had once said to me "Of course it's all right

for you to cheat at tennis isn't it? – because you can go to confession." I often wondered whether any of our uncles and aunts, nineteen all told, had got things wrong to this extent.

At Wittersham there were bound volumes of *Punch* which we loved to browse over, but those over the years round 1850 were full of anti-papist cartoons and jokes of the most virulent kind in which could be detected a forced propaganda hatred. Between ourselves we laughed at them but with a false laughter. It was really rather disturbing to be made aware of such deep-rooted prejudice. Our ally with regard to religion was Aunt Valerie who, being Russian Orthodox, used to go to Mass with us on Sundays, when the car was reluctantly ordered to take us to Rye.

St Anthony's at Rye was a homely little corrugated iron hut, typical of the Catholic Church in England at that time, the cheapness and bad taste in striking contrast with the Latin liturgy. It was served by a Franciscan, and was full of little painted statues of Franciscan saints. After Mass we used to go round to the priest's tiny cottage and talk with him while he ate his breakfast of tea and toast, served by a barefooted lay brother in brown habit. This was real Holy Poverty. What a contrast with Wittersham!

Aunt Valerie was my godmother and I adored her. Whenever she wrote me a letter she addressed me with a long Russian diminutive that went right across the page: 'Klarouchka-oushka-oushouska'. Whenever I went to tea with her, she provided bread rolls and cherry jam, brioches, and coffee éclairs, knowing that to be my idea of a good tea.

She felt homesick for Russia in England and for England in Russia but, like most melancholy people, she had a great sense of humour and though by nature discontented and a grumbler, she gave one a sense of comfort. She once complained all through lunch of a nettle sting on her wrist, saying "You know – the grass that burns," but all the same taking part in the conversation and making jokes between her whines. There was a cosiness about her gentle voice and smiling eyes and she spoke with panting breath in short sentences with a Russian accent – critical and mocking but never wounding.

Aunt Val was smart: she corseted her plump figure well and held it well with a continental carriage, and she knew how to show off a dashing style of dress with dignity. Her hair was yellow and she dressed in beige and yellow ochre colours. She wore Parisian hats with trimmings that went right up in the air; and she always announced her arrival with a loud "Cuckoo!"

When she smoked I couldn't keep my eyes off her. Women rarely smoked before the 1914 war and it was considered rather fast. The Cornish aunts did so occasionally to appear chic, but without achieving the desired effect. They took little puffs and hastily snatched the cigarette from their lips, as though they were afraid of being burned; but Aunt Val knew how to inhale and she set the holder to the side of her mouth to grip it with her teeth as she talked, relapsing into Russian if there was anyone present who could understand. She also knew how to beat the uncles hollow at chess.

Most of the Balfours knew a little Russian, and Bumpa

and Uncle Montie spoke it fluently. At the age of six I used to hold out my mug and say in Russian "Please give me a glass of tea," and I liked the sound of my name in translation: Klara Reginaldova.

When David was eight Mother took him to stay with Uncle Montie at Yoosovka, and while they were away Stephen and I were dumped on our grandparents and many other relations beginning at Wych Cross, the house that our Great Uncle Douglas Freshfield had built in Ashdown Forest. He was Grandmama's brother-in-law and had distinguished himself as a mountaineer – chiefly in the Himalayas. On the morning of David's departure, Stephen and I walked about with him proudly in the garden at Wych Cross and I said to a gardener "Look, this boy is going to Russia," but the gardener paid no attention; he muttered something and went on with his work.

Wych Cross was built in a wonderful position in the heart of Ashdown Forest, but while we were there Nana never allowed us to play in the woods. She was overawed by the grandeur of the house and Mrs English, the housekeeper who ruled it. She walked us solemnly down the drive to the gate and back once a day. I didn't often criticise Nana, but at Wych Cross she seemed smug and I felt that we deserved better than a deadly walk on gravel between shrubs when the forest was all around us. She was not herself there. When Mrs English came to tea in the nursery Stephen and I were tidied up and put on our best behaviour. The conversation was sedate and there were no witticisms from Nana and no laughter.

We sent our letters to Mother in envelopes with the address printed on them in large Russian letters, and she answered us on brightly coloured postcards with scenes of Russian peasant life on which she described her long drives in a sledge drawn by the usual team of three horses known as a 'troika'.

When David came back from Russia, he gave us a rather limited account of his experiences, telling us of his riding lessons and expeditions on a pony with Uncle Montie; but he had been impressed by a Russian officer lifting him up onto the table after dinner and putting a sword in his hand.

My mother's account was more varied. She described the wonderful whistling of Cossacks as they galloped on horseback and the half-wild dogs that guarded the houses, and how the master of the house would walk to his door backwards on getting out of his sledge, whipping them away from him; but David walked up to them without fear, and stroked them. She told us of a Jewish hairdresser who came to cut David's hair in secrecy, crawling through the garden fence, for fear of being seen and losing his life, because the house was out of his bounds; of how surprised she had been on Easter Sunday when an old peasant with a beard had kissed her three times saying "Christ is risen"; and of the peasants who stood outside the churches at the midnight Mass waiting to have their Easter food blessed. She also described the workers coming up from the Yousovka mines and out of the factories, rapidly stripping off their clothes to plunge naked into a swimming pool. I found this very hard to visualise.

Like most houses in Russia, the Balfours' was made

of wood and my mother maintained that she had never before been so warm in winter – even in the sledges which were well provided with foot warmers and fur rugs. She accompanied Valerie on long expeditions to visit neighbours, and this was very agreeable to her as they were all fluent in French and English. The coachman sang as he drove the troika. Once the man had got blind drunk and had driven some horses to death in his frenzy; but he had been forgiven. Nobody seemed to mind how long these visits lasted – they could be prolonged to several days, so timeless was the rhythm of life.

At my grandfather's house an old man used to sit in a corner playing cards and chess all day long. It was said of him, probably with exaggeration, that he had come to a meal many years ago and had stayed on ever since. Mother and David were at Yousovka for the magic moment in the year, so often described by Russian authors, when the ice cracks in frozen rivers, and a sudden thaw sets in. Then the peasants in the neighbouring villages cast off their furs and come out in brightly coloured clothes, barefooted because of the mud, and the air is filled with the sound of the balalaika and accordion.

On their return, we were given many presents – a set of Boyar ninepins, some picture books and wooden toys, and peasant children's clothes. Uncle Montie had given David a balalaika and had taught him to play a few chords on it so that he was able to accompany the Russian song that we learned about a little girl going into a garden to meet a boy: 'Her face was a white little face. Let us not bother about the face'.

This colourful background to my father's family fired me with enthusiasm. One day Aunt Val was going to take me with her to Russia. Alas, this never came about. The Russian Revolution was not only to prevent many plans from being realised but also to break Aunt Valerie's heart. She died in England very soon after the war broke out.

Second to her in my affection came Aunt DD, who was a big and beautiful woman with the same blue eyes and charming voice as Granny. "Beautiful cooing dove," Grandmama called her. She was inclined to sit on the floor and sprawl out on sofas in voluptuous Paolo Veronese positions. She abounded in vitality and had immense powers of enjoyment.

When DD came to Wittersham, an educational atmosphere was introduced and we became less silly. She encouraged us to sing quartets and to play highbrow pencil games; and she took us to see the corn being ground in the windmill. Unfortunately for me the hop harvest was considered very educational. Aunt DD didn't seem to notice the smell and every autumn she took us to visit the oast houses and hop-pickers' camps – sometimes even making us pick hops.

The hop pickers wore London working-class clothes which were quite different from the country people's clothes. They lived in little makeshift shacks like pigsties with sacks of straw and wooden shelves for beds: I never liked to linger for long to watch them. The smell of hops made it all into a nightmare.

Aunt DD was really fond of children and had a way of making one feel appreciated. I was always delighted when she invited me to her bedroom after visiting Granny. One morning as she was talking to me, lying against a pile of pillows, I caught sight of a pink nipple peeping out from a profusion of white lace. I had never seen a breast before and I realised for the first time that a woman's body was beautiful.

Catte, the chauffeur, had a little boy called Georgie with whom we played and of whom we were very fond, and one summer he came to Wittersham with a baby sister. I remember going to see the baby with Aunt Evie in the little cottage by the gate where the family stayed, and being surprised at the way she and Mrs Catte started talking obstetrics and breast feeding on an equal footing, with the freemasonry of women.

The reaction against Victorian prudery had not yet begun and a great wall of secrecy surrounded the subject of sexual functions. Children were kept in total ignorance of such things and even their elders found it hard to call a spade a spade. They referred to many things as 'that nameless horror' and others, more nameable, were given the epithet 'little'. In spite of so much mystery the information had somehow infiltrated into our nursery that babies were fed from their mother's breasts. When we were taken to the National Gallery for the first time, I was surprised to see so many Madonnas depicted with the infant suckling or about to do so. They confirmed the truth of the rumour. David whispered to me "There you are, you see," as we looked at Tintoretto's Milky Way. What an indecent picture it was! When I noticed two young men standing in front of one of these masterpieces in earnest discussion, it never occurred to me that they might be talking of anything but the *subject* of the picture. Then they laughed in public! How could they dare?

And now here was Aunt Evie talking with a social inferior on that forbidden subject in an ordinary voice without casting any looks to the right, left or centre as so many ladies would have done. It was disconcerting to find so many inconsistencies in grown-up behaviour; if only they would stick to the same rules!

Aunt DD was one of the Souls – a group of upper class friends who favoured poetry, cleverness and the pre-Raphaelites – and she had a study of her own at Wittersham that was known as the Blue Room. The walls were painted dark blue and the curtains were pale blue chintz; the writing desk was covered with lapis lazuli objects such as a paper weight, ink well and blotter, and blue flowers were arranged in blue vases. My mother said that it was such a 'boring' idea, but I thought that Aunt DD's blue room was wonderful, and I looked forward to choosing her Christmas presents. You could give Aunt DD blue pencils and india rubbers – even blue blotting paper was acceptable.

The difference between the Cornishes and the Balfours would sometimes be brought home to me with a shock. Apart from her Catholicism my mother was as orthodox in her opinions as could be, and yet the Balfours seemed to think of her as a bohemian. In pre-war England the artist was an outlaw and considered not quite nice to know. The Balfours had one artist friend, an American called Florence Upton. She had a streak of creative genius – she invented the golliwog as a picture book character – but this streak did not appear in her painting. The walls of the dining-room at Wittersham were hung with her portraits of various Balfours and Lytteltons, wearing simpering smiles against eau-de-nil backgrounds (except for Aunt DD's which had been painted in the blue room*. I can remember Aunt DD telling me about Florence Upton's funeral and how, among the many wreaths of flowers that were put on her grave, a little girl had laid a golliwog with a large ribbon round its waist tied in a bow. The golliwog was never patented, so Miss Upton never made a penny out of her invention. She should have made a fortune.

Aunt DD knew many famous intellectuals – actors and producers in particular – and authors who had 'arrived'. People such as Mrs Patrick Campbell, Ellen Terry, and John Buchan were friends of hers. My mother had a friend who was an obscure and rather arty illustrator and that wasn't quite the same thing. Her name was Pamela Coleman Smith.

Pamela had been brought up in the West Indies with coal black mammies as servants, and she used to tell the stories that they had told her as a child – stories about the spider Annancy, Turkel the tortoise, and Toad with the squeaky shoes that went 'Boy-swa, boy-swa.' She told them in the accent and sing-song voice of the negroes, interspersing the narrative with the strange noises that they made and with snatches of song.

*It now hangs in the English-Speaking Union.

My mother had first met her at a party at the G.K. Chestertons, where she had told the stories. When she heard that Pamela was staying at Ellen Terry's house near Wittersham, she suggested that the stories might be a distraction for Granny and she persuaded Bumpa to invite her to lunch with the artist Gordon Craig.

When they arrived – Pamela dressed in a loose embroidered tunic with a scarf round her head instead of a hat, and Gordon Craig in an open shirt and sandals – I felt very ill at ease. The conversation at lunch was one-sided and strained, and Bumpa, from the head of the table, threw out an occasional hearty remark which got little response from the guests.

When lunch was finished we all went into the library where Granny was sitting in her chair and Bumpa went to stand beside her. Pamela took a stool at her feet and began to tell her stories. I loved the Annancy stories but it was impossible to enjoy them under those conditions.

Gordon Craig sat in a corner of the room, isolated and stiff, while a block of unmixable uncles and aunts alternately eyed his sandals and Pamela who, quite unselfconsciously swaying backwards and forwards on her stool, chanted her narrative in a soft and musical voice, occasionally clicking her tongue or bursting into song:

> "You no 'ear ee say Bindila
> You no 'ear ee say Bindila
> You ne 'ear ee say Bindila
> Chichi richi Bindila."

Granny every now and again made a polite little giggle which seemed to express embarrassment rather than amusement at the stories – it was the wrong sort of laugh that suggested the lack of a needed barrier between her and her entertainer. Grandmama Cornish would have been carried away with enthusiasm.

The performance was an agony for me because Pamela was a special nursery friend and here she was not being appreciated. I was very much relieved when she and Gordon Craig left.

At Eton the housework was done by invisible angels (Grandmama and servants) but at Wittersham by human beings who made themselves felt; they were people we knew. Nana had as much respect for the Balfours' servants' hierarchy as for the Roman Curia, and she tried to inspire us with the same awe. It was most unreasonable of her to expect us to call the butler Mr Downes and the housekeeper Miss Ellinger; to us they were simply Downes and Flora.

It was hard to have any respect for Downes. He was a heavy breather with a throaty voice and a pot belly that was accentuated by his striped trousers; and although he had the correct butler's manner, he wore a permanent expression of impertinence on his face.

But Flora did command our respect. Her appearance had a magnetic fascination for me that was tinged with horror; her moustache, her chocolate brown *crêpe-de-chine* gowns, her yellow glacé kid shoes, and the boned net round her neck. It was all horrible and yet an essential part of her, and I liked and admired her. Her voice was whiney and she interrupted her conversation frequently with "Wag 'ee tail: Kwee, Kwee," addressed to her spoilt Persian cat called Brownie, whom we detested. Everything about Flora was elegant, dignified and ugly. Everyone in the house was afraid of her, and she seemed to me to lead a life that was as idle as Granny's.

If Flora could inspire us with awe it can be imagined what effect she had upon Nana.

In the nursery at Wittersham there was a round wooden box, in which biscuits were kept, with a plaque of a cow's head on the lid. My favourite housemaid, Olive, used to make impressions of this bossed head on pieces of tinfoil when she paid a hurried visit to the nursery, and I kept her casts because I thought them most beautiful.

One day Nana told me to take this box to Flora's room with the following instructions: "Tell Miss Ellinger: 'Nana says this is empty,' and say nothing more."

"All right," I answered, "Nana says this is empty – so will you fill it."

"No," Nana said, "on no account must you say that. Just say 'Nana says this is empty.' If you say anything more, you will be punished."

It was one of Flora's few duties to see that the nursery was kept in supply, and Nana was not 'keeping her place' by pointing out her negligence, but I didn't know this. I walked slowly down the passage with the biscuit box in my arms, meditating on the silliness of that message. When I was called into Flora's room I put my lovely box on the floor and knelt down beside it to admire the cow's head. Soon I became aware of Flora looking at me sternly.

I brought myself to say awkwardly, "Nana says this is empty." What an illogical hypocritical message it sounded: "So will you fill it" slipped fatally from my tongue.

I got up from the floor and stood still, absent-mindedly wondering at the innocence of those words and how I could possibly deserve punishment for speaking them. Flora's silence was eloquent, and when I looked at her, she had a very grim look on her face, so I retreated quickly with a fearful sense of guilt.

When I got back to the nursery, the first thing that Nana asked me was "What did you say?"

"'Nana says this is empty'."

"Is that all? Did you say anything else?" she asked with impatient anxiety.

"'So will you fill it' – of course!"

At this Nana's face changed completely, as it did when she was angry; her large mouth puffed out into a 'bull face' and her eyebrows slanted downwards to a fierce frown, and she chased me, crying loudly, out of the room and up to the nursery to be spanked and put to bed.

As we went past Flora's room the door opened and she peeped out to deliver a 'tut-tut' at me, and I thought to myself as I was being rushed upstairs, still crying, 'Wouldn't Nana like her "Miss Ellinger" to know what she is punishing me for?'

We were unusually fortunate in having all four grand-parents alive throughout our childhood. The Eton home was all exquisite beauty, culture and originality. The Wittersham inmates were abounding in generosity, good humour and vitality. The two houses were like strong fortresses, protecting us from the unknown and harmful forces of the outer world.

DORKING

Nursery

MY memories of childhood become consecutive from a definite point, before which they consist of a few isolated impressions; the starting point is scarlet fever in the boys' sanatorium at Eton.

I was sitting on Nana's lap in the little schoolroom in my grandfather's house, feeling ill, and my mother came into the room and said "I thought so." I was carried out of the back door in a blanket and put into a funny little cart with short shafts for a man – a tiny man-drawn ambulance – possibly a tradesman's cart improvised because of infection. Before the door of the cart was shut, my mother assured me that she would be following on a bicycle, and she made the man stop half way to look in at me and see that I was all right.

The time that I spent in the sanatorium was blissful. They had never had a little girl to nurse there before, and I was gloriously spoilt. I acquired a large collection of toys and books, but it was a terrible moment when I saw them put into a lift on the day before my return home to be removed from my sight forever and burned because of infection.

While I was at the sanatorium my mother was moving house. She had bought Cedar House from the dentist at Dorking, choosing to live there on account of her friends the Wards, who had a house called Lotus on the outskirts of the town, and the Gibsons at Moorhurst nearby.

Cedar House was early Victorian – with a little cedar tree (gigantic to us) in the middle of the garden and an orchard in which Rascal the donkey was kept, with a dovecote at the end.

My mother in her widowhood thought of herself as very poor and yet that little house contained several servants hidden away behind green baize doors; and the nursery quarters were a separate institution. When I arrived at Dorking the family could only have been settled in for a few days, but they gave me the impression of having lived there for ages, and I felt out of it. I found my brothers and sister digging a grave under the cedar tree for Dinah the cat who was in the prime of life and excellent condition. I felt frightened for Dinah and didn't like to ask why she needed a grave.

We were soon summoned in from the garden by Nana clapping her hands and were given our tea in a tiny room called the servants' hall, where a full-length photograph of Pius X hung on the wall. I thought he looked like some old

lady we knew. Was it Great Aunt Minnie? No, it was Great
Aunt Margie. When I asked a tentative question about 'her'
I came in for a volley of snubs from Hester and David. Didn't
I know who the Pope was? Couldn't I see his tiara? Wasn't
I a Catholic? I decided to be more careful with my questions.

Although Cedar House was tiny, the grown-up world
was separated from ours and rather enfolded in mystery.
I always longed for more of Mother's company and to go
out with her was a rare treat. She seemed inaccessible so
that her life had an element of romance for me. I sometimes
looked out of the nursery window to watch her moving
about in the garden, tall and graceful. I thought she looked
like a princess in a fairy story and wished that I could walk
among the flower beds with her.

Every day at Cedar House we were made to change after
tea into muslin frocks or white ducks for the boys before
going down to the little drawing-room. Hester and I had
coral necklaces clasped round our necks, and our hair was
tied up with satin ribbons to match the sashes round our
waists. This dressing for the drawing-room seemed endless,
and every knot in my hair that Nana pulled at was a
precious moment wasted that might have been spent with
Mother, a moment in a part of the day that I so much
enjoyed. I used to wonder why there was so much ceremony
to separate us from her. The reason was that it was soon
after my father's death and she found us a strain; she was
also ill at that time. Children of my generation saw little
enough of their parents but we saw less than most of our
mother and, as a result, servants played a very important
part in our lives.

Behind a green baize door worked Ada, the flighty cook, who sometimes came up to the nursery to show herself off to Nana before going out on her day off. Ada was one of the few people whose clothes gave me pleasure. She had a Toulouse-Lautrec silhouette and a Pearly Queen glamour, and she wore enormous flowered hats and feather boas. Although I knew that her trappings were cheap, I thought that her get-up was wonderful and I liked to imagine her behaving with dashing style at the dances she went to – foxtrotting to the tune that was the rage then:

> Everybody's doing it, doing it,
> Everybody's doing it, doing what?
> The Turkey Trot.

She was the origin of our nursery expression 'Ada Lady' which we applied to any flirtatious and frivolous female.

Ada never stayed for long in the nursery and never came there in her working clothes. Miss Crabbe, the dress-maker, on the other hand, did her sewing there and ate her meals with us. Even at little Cedar House the conventions of a staff were respected as a duty towards the making of an ordered society, and everybody had their proper place.

Miss Crabbe had first appeared in the family at Eton in 1900 to make my mother's trousseau and, since then, had been summoned by each of the Warre Cornishes for every wedding and as upholsteress for every house move. When my father died she turned up on the doorstep on her own initiative to make my mother's mourning.

Miss Crabbe was tall and thin and had the voice and movements of a deaf person. She spoke in little jerky sentences: "Must have a good meal mid-day," or "Go to the shop. Get some thread." She and Nana were the greatest of friends, and I used to wonder how it was that they got so much pleasure from telling the same stories over and over again. Miss Crabbe used to bend over Nana with her hands on her knees putting her best ear to Nana's mouth.

Dressing the four of us took up quite a lot of her time. Hester and I were always turned out as a pair in slightly French clothes designed by Mother. The boys were usually in sailor suits – and we all wore blue pinafores for playing in the garden.

I was the only one in the family not possessed of striking good looks – Nana called me the "ugly ducking" – but in spite of this I was able to enjoy the admiration that was so often showered on us collectively in Dorking as an attractive family in the charge of the little nanny who was such a character. We were noticed when she took us out on a daily walk, dressed in our four grey tweed coats with black bands of mourning round the sleeves. Miss Crabbe fitted up Hester and me in black satin outfits, copies from a portrait of Queen Victoria as a little girl when she was in mourning. We wore black hats to match, with broad ribbons spread across the brims. (Queen Victoria's hat was trimmed with black ostrich feathers.)

I loved going to church with Mother in this outfit, looking at my white socks and patent leather shoes as I walked beside her, and I felt far too proud of my clothes to mind being jeered at by David as 'Queen Victoria'.

We had been told that Daddy was in heaven and when we said the Our Father I imagined that we were praying to him. I wondered how other people said that prayer. Did they say 'The Balfours' Father'? I listened carefully in church but no, they all prayed to Daddy as if he was theirs too. It was very strange.

Whereas the family friends in Sussex were all of a literary bent, the Dorking neighbours were more interested in philosophy and theology.

Wilfrid Ward, editor of the *Dublin Review* and a prominent Catholic writer at that time, was a genial man with a grey beard and was very fond of children. We called him 'Jabberwock' and he used to greet us by sitting down at the piano to sing a song about a merry little fat grey man. His four children were considerably older than us but always ready to enjoy our company, and Lotus, presided over by the intellectual Aunt Jo*, was a very gay and cosy home in spite of the family passion for Catholic apologetics. The eldest daughter, Maisie, was later to marry Frank Sheed and with him to found the publishing firm of Sheed and Ward. The youngest son, Leo, was to become a priest.

Wilfrid Ward's family owned property in the Isle of Wight so he shared some of Mother's background in the Tennysons' circle of friends at Farringford. Maisie could remember going for a walk as a little girl with Tennyson and her father when the bard had suddenly said to her "Just run on ahead, dear, for a little while, will you? I want to tell your father a dirty story."

The other friends of my mother's in Dorking whom we often visited were William and Marie-Anne Gibson†. They had no children, but we loved their house, Moorhurst, where they bred rabbits and pigeons and kept aquaria full of rare fish as well as many pets – at one time they even had a bear cub.

They were both converts to Catholicism, he being Northern Irish and she a French Protestant by birth, and they were both rather eccentric. In her girlhood Marie-Anne had been much influenced by a puritanical English governess who condemned the frivolities of the world and inspired her with a desire to join the Salvation Army to convert France to Protestantism. Marie-Anne was reluctant

*Née the Hon. Josephine Hope-Scott.
†Later Lord and Lady Ashbourne.

and rebellious and she refused to wear fashionable clothes, especially if they were *décolleté*.

There was in Paris at that time a priest called Abbé Huvelin who was a man of remarkable insight and wisdom[*]. He had been rather taken up by society on this account. Although she was a Protestant, Marie-Anne's mother, the Comtesse de Montbrison, decided to take her to him to ask his advice.

They drove together in silence in the family carriage to his presbytery and were shown into a tiny unheated room furnished only with *prie-dieux* on which they crouched. When the holy man came in, he bade them remain seated and he stood still in the middle of the room silently for several minutes with his eyes shut. Then he spoke, addressing Marie-Anne; "You are making your parents very unhappy," and he summed up their situation. Mother and daughter listened with tears dripping onto their muffs as he spoke, begging Marie-Anne to submit to her parents' wishes on a trial of one year. She agreed, and put off joining the Salvation Army; but though she went to balls in the special modest creations that her mother ordered from Parisian couturiers, she declined every offer to dance.

The Comtesse – knowing that eligible aristocratic French protestants were very few – took her two daughters the following summer to do the London season. Of all the young men they met, the very serious William Gibson, heir

[*]Abbé Huvelin has since become famous for the part he played in the conversion of Charles de Foucauld, the mystic and desert hermit. The two men were to correspond until Huvelin's death in 1911.

to an Irish barony who always had some volume of heavy reading tucked under his arm, seemed to be the most suitable for the earnest Marie-Anne, in revolt against the frivolity of the fashionable world. William Gibson's courtship was well advanced before Madame de Montbrison realised that he had just become a Catholic. As Marie-Anne was French it had not occurred to him that she might be anything else and he was horrified when she told him that her highest ambition was to join the Salvation Army and convert France to Protestantism. However, in course of time Marie-Anne changed her mind and followed him into the Church, instructed by the Abbé Huvelin.

Poor Mme de Montbrison – her plans didn't quite come off. Her other daughter, Jacqueline, married an aristocratic Protestant Frenchman, but he made her so unhappy that she quickly divorced him in favour of a Russian Orthodox Count, and that was blissful.

Marie-Anne was a very good artist and painted instinctively in the technique of the Impressionists whose work she had never seen. The private chapel at Moorhurst was decorated by her with scenes from the Gospel and portrayals of many saints, for which her husband had evidently served as a model: there he was as St Michael in a kilt casting out Satan, as St Patrick, St Joseph and – most embarrassingly naked – as St Sebastian. He himself would kneel in his chapel in the evening to lead the prayers of the rosary with the Irish servants (both he and the gardener in kilts) answering behind him. We knew how to pray in Latin but Gaelic was too much for us. This is what the 'Hail Mary' sounded like:

Shall I bang you a banana you little Moloty?
I'll bang you a banana Bathoragen, yes!

A childish spontaneity made Marie-Anne accessible to
us and she remained a friend of mine until she died in 1953.

William Gibson, as a pioneer of the Gaelic League,
usually wore the saffron kilt of the Irish Guards and
sometimes Druid's robes. A Benedictine or Franciscan
guest in his habit often completed the impression of a fancy
dress party. Edwardian gentlemen were histrionic and fond
of dressing up at home in the clothes appropriate to the
cause that they championed, and it was not unusual for the
master of a house to be seen on a grass lawn drinking tea
poured from a silver teapot, and wearing a kaftan or some
garment designed to keep out desert sands.

Gibson's theology tended to be eccentric like his dress.
At one time the American flag was flying over Moorhurst
because of his enthusiasm for a movement called
Americanism. When the doctrine was condemned as a
heresy the flag was hauled down. He was a follower of the
modernists and a close friend of Father Tyrrell's*. Both at
Moorhurst and at Lotus metaphysical speculation was
continuous; both the Gibsons and the Wards had the same

*Fr George Tyrrel SJ got into trouble early in his career with the Roman
Curia on account of the modernistic trend of his writings. He was finally
forbidden to say Mass and asked to leave the Jesuits, but was not
excommunicated. He ended his days at Storrington and was buried
there. Among the few mourners at his funeral was William Gibson.
Another was Baron Friedrich von Hügel, the son of an Austrian Diplomat
by an English mother, a philosopher and author of *The Mystical Element
in Religion*.

zest for controversy and they seemed to enjoy it as much as we did our nursery nonsense.

One day Herbie Ward came up to the nursery and talked politics with Nana heatedly while we ate our tea. When he had left the room Hester said: "I don't see why Ireland should have Home Rule," and this set Nana off onto a long political tirade, at the end of which she asked "Now do you see why?" Hester replied "No, I don't see Wye. The Wallipug lives in Wye." (The Wallipug of Wye was the hero of a picture book.) At this Nana jumped up and chased Hester out of the room, but she came back to sit on her chair and laugh with us till she had to take off her spectacles to dry her eyes. That pun of Hester's earned her the reputation of a brilliant nursery wit.

Our nursery was a world in itself. We invented our own language and customs. Our meals were made interesting by a lot of little ceremonies. Every morning Nana dressed us in coats and hats and sent us out into the garden to get an appetite while she prepared the breakfast, and this was called our 'appetite run'. Part of our breakfast consisted of sandwiches divided into triangles which, cut out from a cottage loaf, had the shape of kites. We called them 'appetite kites' and made them fly about in the air before landing them in our mouths. We decided that when we ate bananas their souls ascended to heaven after we had consumed their flesh, and we looked up at the ceiling to direct them on their celestial flight – the banana skins on our plates made convincing corpses.

But the best nursery ritual was invented by Michael MacCarthy, our cousin. He decided that a milk pudding was so disgusting as to be not only uneatable but also unseeable, and whenever one was put on the table he gave the order: "Pull up your blinds!" whereupon the MacCarthy children all threw their bibs back over their faces. The milk pudding, considered then to be essential to a child's health, was the cause of untold misery, especially tapioca pudding.

Nana's contribution to our nursery lore was the 'bull face game'. It consisted of her chasing us round the nursery table, puffing out her cheeks and snorting, which made us shriek with laughter. I was never frightened of her then, and I knew that she was only pretending to be a bull, but in the early morning Nana was a wolf. As she was dressing, before Stephen and I got up, I used to turn my head to the wall for fear of seeing her. She stood at the wash-stand on which she kept a jar of oatmeal for her ablutions, and cleared her throat a lot. Her grey hair hung loose from her head, and she wasn't wearing spectacles. I once caught sight of a loose grey breast. I didn't dare to look at the wolf and never started talking to Stephen until Nana was fully dressed with her hair piled up on her head and she was herself again. I never knew if Stephen shared my fear and I never spoke of it. He used to lie in bed silent and still like me while she was dressing.

One day we went down to the drawing-room to meet a priest who had a beard. He took me on his knee and gave me a rather Byzantine-looking holy picture of three saints standing in a row. I asked him why they all had hats on, and he explained the symbolism of the halo, giving the name of each saint. Then I pointed to a little bird above them that wore a halo too, and asked him if he was a saint. The priest said "No, but he makes saints," and he talked about the Holy Ghost. I loved that little bird! I imagined him in a little workshop mixing plaster and paint with his beak and sawing bits of wood with his wings to make statues, then he blew on them and they became alive. After this my fancy ran away with me. I thought that I could guess how living things were made. I had seen horses with their manes and tails plaited in brightly coloured braid and imagined that the braid slowly turned into horse hair.

One early morning Stephen and I went out for our appetite run and looked into the field beyond the garden. It was a frosty morning and we opened our mouths wide to see our misty breath. In the field a farmer was sawing bits of wood while some sheep stood in a row to watch him, like us. I told Stephen that the farmer would make a wooden model of a sheep, that he would then blow on it to make it move, after which some wool would begin to grow on its back. Everything was made like that in a kind of toy factory.

Stephen believed me and repeated my lesson at breakfast, but his information was categorically contradicted by Hester and David. They couldn't tell us how sheep were made, but it certainly was not like that. Their snubs brought me down to earth again – and I began to realise that my fantasies took me too far, but I loved my little picture of the Holy Ghost. I took it to bed with me and gloated over it. I fancied that I saw the bird moving in the picture.

It was the same as in the book that the nurses read aloud to me in the sanatorium, changing the names to those of my own family. There was a picture in it that I particularly liked of the girl that they called Hester. She was standing at the foot of the staircase in her nightgown holding a bedroom candlestick. When I shut the book she went up the stairs inside it, and this was an event that was repeated over and over again which I was never able to see.

I had the same sort of impression when I first discovered that I could read. But then I did get inside the book.

We were taught our first lessons from a book called *Reading without Tears*, with late Victorian illustrations. The letters were turned into figures: 'd' was said to be like a lady walking forwards and was incorporated into a picture of a lady with a bustle, and for the 'b' the lady turned her bustle the other way and the letter was said to be like a lady walking backwards. As bustles were long out of fashion these illustrations did not make much impression. After struggling for a long time with these inappropriate picture letters I was introduced to a different method at school and suddenly found myself reading and entering a new world.

I was sitting on the nursery floor with my legs stuck out and this book on my lap, and the miracle happened in a second. I found myself reading, and as I read I got inside the book. I seemed to be climbing over the words to reach a dog called Tray in the top corner of the page: he was a white dog with red patches and floppy ears. I talked to him, and moved down to the next line with him. I shouted with joy, and David and a nursery maid came and stooped over me as I slowly read out my first few words.

During the years at Dorking I was at the age of mastery of the elementary skills. It was there that I first learnt to whistle, to catch a ball, and laboriously lace up my boots. They were the years during which the child emerges from the land of visions, groping and blinking, to explore a more tangible world.

I remember having a conversation with Uncle Desmond when I was in my twenties about different periods in one's life and him saying "I don't suppose, Clare, that for you anything has quite come up to Dorking." He was probably right. I can remember him saying to me another time that he believed everybody had one best time in their life.

LONDON

Schoolroom

IN the spring of 1912 we went to live in London permanently and had the great excitment of moving to our new home, 3 Berkeley Gardens on Campden Hill. I slept for the first time in a little room of my own. A new life was to begin and I felt very grown up. Mother made her drawing-room on the first floor by knocking two rooms into one, with windows and flower-decked balconies at each end, and she had glass-paned bookcases built, painted all in a blue green that was her favourite colour. I so often heard her guests tell her that it was the prettiest room in London that I thought it must be true.

Though Nana was still with us the word 'nursery' was dropped for our living room and substituted by 'school-room'. We were Londoners and the place was ours.

3 Berkeley Gardens

Soon after we had settled in, Hester and David were invited with Mother to stay with some Balfour cousins called Donaldson Hudson at their house, Cheswardine Hall, in Shropshire. David, who had never met these cousins before, thought hard for some way of impressing them on his arrival and he had a brain wave on the morning of their departure. He found a blue tiddlywink and had the idea that, if he sucked off the paint, his mouth would remain blue till the end of the long journey and after several meals. He planned that when they arrived at Cheswardine he would say to Michael Donaldson Hudson "What colour is the inside of your mouth? Mine's blue," and he would put out his tongue. While he was turning the tiddlywink round in his mouth to get every part of it thoroughly blued, it slipped down his throat and got stuck there. He came rushing downstairs, saying very fast "I've swallowed a tiddlywink. I've swallowed a tiddlywink," and making an hysterical noise like the whinneying of a horse. Mother put on her hat and quickly took him to the nearest doctor round the corner, and while they were away the cab that was to take them to the station arrived at the door. Presently we heard the whinneying again and Mother stamping up and down the hall, talking about "That fool of a doctor." He had pushed the tiddlywink down David's throat still further where it had got stuck more firmly, and she was giving orders and counter orders for putting the luggage on and off the cab.

As soon as they got back, Nana had taken David into the bathroom next to the schoolroom and held his head over the wash basin to try to make him throw up the tiddlywink.

I joined with him in retching as I sat at my breakfast, listening to the horrible noises from next door. But the retching brought no result, and Mother ordered the luggage to be taken off the cab and planned to take David in it to her own doctor.

Nana, in the meantime, had dragged David back into the schoolroom, plumped him down on a chair, and imperatively but with perfect calm had begun to push spoonfuls of porridge into his mouth. Then suddenly he stopped his noise, jumped up from his chair, and was violently sick on the floor. We all watched a discoloured tiddlywink roll round in a circle on the blue linoleum, and then we all burst out laughing. As soon as Mother heard of this she quickly ordered the luggage to be put onto the cab again and bundled Hester and David into it. The cabby whipped up his horse, and they rushed off to the station, without having had any breakfast, to catch the train by the skin of their teeth. Nana kept the discoloured tiddlywink as a memento in a little china box on the nursery mantleshelf and a new story was added to those endlessly repeated between her and Miss Crabbe and other cronies. "I forced it [the porridge] down you know," she used to say.

After that visit to Shropshire, Stephen and I had to listen to long talks between Hester and David about the Donaldson Hudson cousins whom we had never met. Ruth and Michael, Twinks and John, seemed to be children who excelled at every sport and Cheswardine sounded like a glorious amusement park, and we waited for a second invitation which never came.

London was a familiar place long before we went to live there because our Balfour grandparents' house was in Knightsbridge and they liked to gather their large family round them in their house in newly-built Pont Street.

Osbert Lancaster classified that style of architecture as 'Pont Street Dutch'. An enormous lot was sacrificed by the architect to make the façade look like that of a house on an Amsterdam canal, behind which the requirements of Edwardian family life had to be provided for. This meant allowing ample room in depth so that the rooms had uncomfortable proportions and the middle of the house was very dark. The windows were of an Amsterdam height but remarkable for their poverty of outlook.

The portrait of Great Grandfather Weguelin with mutton chop whiskers was in the darkest recess of the hall, hanging opposite a full-length portrait of my grandmother and her brother, Christopher, as children, dressed alike, both *décolleté* in crinolines and pantaloons with golden curls kissing their cheeks. I couldn't believe it when I was told that one of them was a boy. In the dining-room all the sideboards displayed a collection of bronze statuettes of Cossacks on horseback in lively and realistic movement.

The first important London event that I can remember is Uncle Duggie's wedding, at which Hester was a bridesmaid. We went up from Dorking and, for the ceremony, Stephen and I sat in the gallery of the church with Nana and the Balfour servants. The procession walked up the aisle, the bride followed by little girls in dresses of cream brocade with Dutch caps on their heads. After some mumbling between the couple and the clergyman, Uncle Duggie took his bride to a door at the side of the altar and it closed behind them. There was a sense of relaxation in the church and Olive, the first housemaid, said audibly "Ah! Now they're going to sign the register." I didn't know what this meant but I imagined that something very intimate and indelicate was going on behind that door – Aunt Hilda was being laid in her bridal gown on a kind of doctor's couch and some secret rite was being performed. While they were away the bridesmaids collected in a little group and we could see Hester in all her glory. Mary Lyttelton, the eldest, turned round to the others and they chatted and laughed together. Hester seemed to be in a wonderful and inaccessible world, enjoying the wittiest jokes – but in fact they had been set off laughing by Mary saying to each one in turn "Hullo, bridesmaid's cap!"

Then the vestry door opened and Uncle Duggie reappeared with our new aunt on his arm. They were both smiling, and the procession out of the church was wonderful. There was Hester and Cecilia beside her and the three Paget girls (first cousins, daughters of Christopher Balfour) with Mary following behind – a troupe of fairy princesses. When we got out into the street Nana called out to the butler "Our turn next, Mr Downes!" and gave a great cackle of laughter.

My mother in no way had what is known as a social life – a dinner engagement for her was rare. Like her own mother she exacted the first rate, and superficial sociability depressed her. But every now and again – suddenly, on the spur of the moment – she would give a party such as a hard working *salonnière* might have taken years to achieve.

Donald Tovey would come to London and Hilaire Belloc, delighting in his witticisms on the piano, never liked to miss a chance of meeting him. If both chanced to come together, Maurice Baring would automatically appear (perhaps after an absence of years) and Uncle Desmond (MacCarthy) was always willing to join them. With those four as a nucleus Chesterton would sometimes come, and other friends foregather. Then good food, good wine, and good talk abounded.

At an early age Hester and I, in white muslin frocks, were allowed an occasional glimpse of these celebrations. That generation were given to childish jocularity and chaffing and to practical jokes. "Oh! poor Bear," Belloc would say "have you hurt your paw?" when Edmund Warre (nicknamed the Bear) spilt some hot coffee on his hand. Then he would tell the story of the Duke who got onto a 'bus and said "Home," to the conductor, or of the conversation between two men in a railway carriage; how one said that he didn't believe in ghosts and the other answered "Well, as a matter of fact I am a ghost," and disappeared.

Donald would be compulsively drawn to the piano and would play some of Belloc's verses for which he had made settings: 'E stands for egg', to loud Wagnerian chords, followed by 'F for a family taking a walk', with a perambulatory accompaniment. And he illustrated the story of two rival opera singers meeting on the doorstep of a composer who was in need of a bass capable of unusually low notes. One man sang this question to the other: "Are you the man with the deep bass voice?"

The answer: "Yes, I'm the man with the deep bass voice," was sung to the same notes an octave lower by Tovey with the help of the piano.

Maurice could play a whole mock sonata – with changes of movement and the gestures of a concert pianist – consisting entirely of discords.

Once, on seeing Donald off in the hall, I asked him if he had an umbrella and he said "I can't afford a new umbrella every time it rains." These gatherings would come about once in a blue moon; they were always unpremeditated and invariably the greatest success.

What we enjoyed most was going to the MacCarthys' house in Wellington Square, which in those days was a humble square. The eighteenth-century houses in old Chelsea Village near the river had always been the homes of the intellectual élite, but Victorian Chelsea was not yet fashionable, and Peter Jones was then a small draper's store.

The table in the hall of the MacCarthys' house was always covered with parcels of books, and very often a black wide-brimmed hat, such as were worn at that time by men of letters, lay among them. Perhaps Lytton Strachey had called, or one of his set, for which Aunt Molly had coined the name 'Bloomsbury'. It was at this house that the first meetings of the Memoir Club were held, a club founded by her in collaboration with Virginia Woolf. The original membership included Duncan Grant, Clive and Vanessa Bell, Maynard Keynes and E.M. Forster, in addition to the Woolfs and the MacCarthys. They met once a month to read aloud a memoir written by one of themselves for discussion and criticism – often, it is said, to hoots of laughter. Aunt Molly had hoped that these gatherings might lead to Uncle Desmond writing a book in addition to his articles. In fact their best result was a small masterpiece of her own, *A Nineteenth Century Childhood*, first published by Hamish Hamilton, and still in print after fifty years.

The house seemed to be bursting with books. Every recess of each room had in it a bookcase made to its measurement, however narrow, and so did every landing. As you went upstairs the books became more and more numerous, until the top floor where they spilled out of Uncle Desmond's study like a waterfall, with piles of them on either side of each tread of the stairs.

Years later, in the hall at Wellington Square, I once came

upon Uncle Desmond as an old man picking up a parcel from the table. He told me then, that in spite of his long years of drudgery as a reviewer, it still gave him pleasure to untie the string in anticipation of the book inside the wrapping.

MAINLY LONDON

Education

WHEN I was young the only thing aimed at in the bringing up of girls was 'tone'. Though my mother was critical of the education that she had had from Miss Weisse (so much more thorough than mine) she was full of the negative prejudices then prevailing.

A girl was expected to speak French really well, and one or two other languages tolerably (but not more than two). She should be able to play the piano – perhaps a second instrument could be allowed – and know how to sing in parts and at sight.

A wide but unthorough reading of the English classics was to be encouraged and learning poetry by heart. A few landmarks in history had to be grasped, but the rest was deliberately planned as a light skim on the surface, except for embroidery, gardening and horses, on which subjects a thorough knowledge was allowed.

I was sent for a time to a convent in Hampstead on three days of the week only (three non-hockey days and without a school uniform) so that my education should be kept nice and sketchy. This was against my will because I loved school; and at home there was the unnatural situation of a child clamouring for more lessons and more discipline and being denied them for no understandable reason.

I walked in a crocodile of navy-blue girls wearing a plum coloured coat with a highwayman's collar, beside a girl called Olga Tchitchagoff who told me stories about Russia. I enjoyed every minute of these three days and made myself popular with the girls by singing David's comic songs.

I went to school by the 31 bus, which took me to Hampstead by way of the Paddington slums. In the evening the streets swarmed with children – chiefly little boys possessed of enormous energy. In those days of horse traffic they were expert at jumping onto the backs of moving carts to get a clandestine ride, free and unobserved, and they roller skated on the road. They also did wonderful trapese acts in the gaps between broken railings or on ropes tied across an open front door. Hop-scotch and whip tops (games for some reason denied to upper class children) were kept going non-stop on the pavement.

I envied these little boys their freedom, but pitied them for the clothes they had to wear. Many of them were dressed in lopped men's trousers into which they almost disappeared, and their feet were shod with any kind of gear of any shape or size, very often women's high-heeled boots.

The mothers stood in groups at their doors chatting with the neighbours, or sat on the steps nursing their babies with as little shame of exposing the body as their half-clad young sons. Most of them had men's caps pinned onto their buns, with high-heeled button boots on their feet; and they all wore pinafores patterned with tiny flowers, even under their overcoats.

This was a world on its own – a remote world with which there seemed no possibility of contact – and having a glimpse of it gave an additional interest to going to school; but the glimpses didn't last for long. Even the three days a week were thought to be making me too schoolgirlish so they were stopped and, as Hester was not very happy at her boarding-school, she came home to have private lessons with me.

A governess called Elizavieta Ivanova came every day to teach us Russian. She was prim and rather melancholy but she knew it and invited us to laugh at her own dreary character, but in spite of this admitted dreariness she managed to inspire us with enthusiasm for Russian folk lore, singing peasants' songs in her thin little voice and doing their dances with stiff movements.

Under her influence I became an ardent Russophile and I walked in Kensington Gardens with an imaginary borzoi called Moujik at my heels.

Whenever Aunt Valerie came to lunch she used to tease Elizavieta Ivanova in Russian and pinch her behind to make her blush – all of which helped to build up an excellent relationship between teacher and pupils. Except for Russian, French and the 'cello, all school subjects were temporarily abandoned.

At that time I met my cousin Ann Talbot in Kensington Gardens, and I hated the thought of her knowing about my eccentric education. When I saw her coming towards me I prayed that she wouldn't ask me about it, but the dreaded questions came immediately.

What school was I at? – None. What was I doing at home? – Learning French, Russian, and the 'cello.

I racked my brains for a change of subject – if only that could be her last question – but I was too late to avert it. Was I doing anything else? I had to say "no," and confess to the extremest oddity.

When she was in Russia my mother had been much impressed by the education of the children she had met – their mastery of foreign languages in particular. They were taught by resident tutors and made to speak in a different language each day, only addressing the servants and peasants in Russian.

This was very much in keeping with her own ideas on education. She made us ride our first pony with a jockey's saddle to make sure that we would fall off in the right way; and, having had us taught the Eton swimming stroke, she didn't go so far as to throw us into the water, but she let us fend for ourselves without any further help.

On her return to England from Russia, my mother had decided that we should make a start in three languages on the Russian principle, with daily governesses. A middle-aged Fraülein, an elderly Signorina, and a very young Mademoiselle were engaged to come and teach us – each on two days of the week – and to take us out for a walk in Kensington Gardens for conversation after a lesson in grammar.

We went down the flights of stairs on Monday and Thursday with the Signorina counting "*Uno, due, tre,*" on Tuesday and Friday with the Fraülein counting "*Ein, zwei, drei*". The Mademoiselle was engaged to come on Wednesday and Saturday, which were to be the *un, deux, trois* days.

I have no idea how long the Fraülein and the Signorina lasted – we at least learnt how to count up to ten in Italian and German – but the Mademoiselle's day was a short one, in point of fact half a day, and it nearly cost me my life.

We went down the stairs with her counting them in French up to "*dix*", then somebody said "Knave, queen, king," which spread an infectious hilarity among us, and once inside Kensington Gardens it was clear who was going to have the upper hand, Mademoiselle or us.

Mademoiselle spoke to us in French and very fast, and as we didn't understand her we began to giggle. What was worse, she found our giggles infectious and seemed to be amused at her own lack of authority. We rushed about wildly, deliberately disobeying the notices to keep the public off the grass and we decided that if a park keeper were to protest, we would pretend to be foreigners and speak to him in gibberish.

The little Mademoiselle got desperate, rushing after us in all directions and reproving us in French. I asked David to translate *Qu'est ce que c'est que ça!* for me and he told me, with an air of authority, that it meant 'Go on doing what you're doing!' and Mademoiselle never changed her form of reproof. At last I jumped over some high railings and rolled about on the wet grass in front of a flower bed.

Mademoiselle ran towards me and delivered a volley of *qu'est ce que c'est que ça*'s at me while the others stood in a row roaring with laughter. Inspired by their applause I went on and on 'doing what I was doing'.

Then a kind French-speaking lady came to the rescue of the poor little governess. She made us all four hold hands and took us to the park gate where she left us; it must have been long before the time appointed for the end of our walk.

I was still feeling over-excited and naughty and, while we were standing in a row on the edge of the pavement, I slipped Mademoiselle's hand and started to cross the road by myself. When I got to the island half way across, I looked back and saw a look of terror on the faces of my brothers and sister, a look of fury on the face of a bus driver as he jammed on his brakes and, on all sides, anxious and indignant grown-ups came to a halt to watch my perilous progress across the road.

Things had gone too far. The walk home was sober and penitent, and that governess was never seen again.

WHEN I was seven I spent one term at the convent at Ascot where Hester was then a boarder, to make my first communion, and this made a great impression on me.

A nun called Sister Ignatius instructed me and I was filled with religious fervour. She described the Passion to me in such a way as to make me see suffering as a wonderful thing.

At meals I sat next to an Irish girl called Guitha, who told me that her grandmother was a real saint, the proof being that she had seen a statue move. This made me feel jealous. My father, I thought, had been a saint but I could not prove it. Had he ever seen a statue move? When I asked Mother she burst out laughing. I was disconcerted.

I adored boarding-school life. I found the girls, the nuns, the games, the lessons, everything – even the rules – of absorbing interest and I hadn't any criticism to make whatsoever.

But Mother did not want me to go to school because, in a way, it suited me only too well. I was a good scholar but there was a prevailing prejudice against learned women who were branded as blue stockings. My mother was afraid of my becoming 'schoolgirlish', and she couldn't have borne a 'blue stocking' daughter.

One summer term during a quarantine we went to Devon for a few weeks. To my envy Stephen was sent trotting off on a pony to a clergyman in plus fours, who coached him in Latin. For a girl to do this would have been unthinkable.

Much later, when David was about twelve, I remember his arguing with Mother "Why should I learn Greek? None of the other boys do."

"A classical education is a family tradition," she told him, "and the basis of a good education."

'Yes, but only for boys', I thought. My education was deliberately planned to skim lightly the surface of learning.

LONDON, for us, meant Campden Hill and Chelsea.

The Campden Hill centre of children's social life was the house that George Booth had built for his family of six. We were connected with them several times over and joined the many gatherings of cousins there, for plays, children's

orchestras (the Booths all played musical instruments), dances and concert parties – all enormously enjoyable. Our sorties to Chelsea were also frequent because so many relations lived there. I often went to see Peggy at her father's house in Cheyne Walk, and there were the Edmund Fishers (also our second cousins) in Swan Walk, where Stephen and I attended a weekly dancing class dressed in our best party clothes. Great Aunt Annie lived in St Leonard's Terrace and there we went to play with her grandchildren. I felt the charm of Aunt Annie's personality from an early age – an old lady with a lace cap on her head, which she held a little to one side.

The MacCarthys very often came to us at Berkeley Gardens too and together we founded an exclusive cousins' club of which I was a domineering president. We called it the Chough Club because the crest of the Cornish family is a chough.

The membership of our club was no more than eight: Stephen and I, Michael and Rachel, Francis and Philip Cornish, and Ros and Racy Fisher; but we made elaborate rules, chose *noms de plume*, and held meetings about nothing whatever. All of this was an enjoyable waste of time, but the Chough Club did produce a magazine, with Stephen as editor, and it had some excellent entries: romantic drawings of mediaeval scenes by Francis, poems by his little brother Philip, and fantastic imcomprehensible contributions from Rachel. I wrote a story about Exmoor ponies in the Ernest Thompson Seton style beginning 'Oh life! Oh freedom!' and a serial Dickensian novel with a hero called Peter Merrivale who was stabbed secretly by a gipsy mother; but the instalments didn't extend to the clearing up of her mystery.

We acted many plays that I wrote with Mother's help. One was based on a Russian fairy story, and Elizavieta Ivanova painted the scenery for it. I took the part of the witch, Baba Iaga, who rides about on a mortar pushing herself along with a pestle.

Grandmama came to the dress rehearsal and watched me propelling myself about in a cardboard contraption as I chanted:

> "Oh, mortar mortar carry me
> And pestle strong and sound
> Push me hard and fast, while broom,
> Sweep traces off the ground."

She was horrified at my grimaces and said to me afterwards at tea: "You know, Clare, you should turn your face more to the audience – your pretty face because, you know, witches are pretty." I was not influenced by her criticism; I thought it was just Grandmama's ridiculous nonsense and I went on making ugly faces.

Another memorable play was the life of St Francis (my great hero) with Pamela Coleman Smith in the part of a leper and Hester (dreary as usual) as a Lady Poverty all in rags. Bumpa came to the first performance and I tried not to catch his eye in the audience lest it should cramp my style, but when it was over he patted me on the back and said "Jolly good, old girl," and at the tea-party after the play I smoked a cigarette in my brown habit, partly to counteract the religious atmosphere, but chiefly to show off.

For these performances my mother was always the stage manager and under her direction I was able to throw myself wholeheartedly into my part. She was an inspiring coach, but when I acted away from home (as I often did with the Booths and other cousins) I found the rehearsals intimidating and stultifying and it was not until my final performance that the manager and cast were often surprised; I didn't mind how much my first awkwardness was despised – I knew that I could steal the show when it came to the point and I bided my time.

On our walks in Kensington Gardens we often met Baron von Hügel, the Catholic philosopher, exercising his naughty Pekinese.

I see him in my memory always in the same position – bending forwards with his hands outstretched and his

Inverness cape flapping round him as he rushed about between the wooden hoops and pram wheels to catch his little dog. When he had it securely leashed, he used to take off his billicock to make a formal bow to Minjou, and sometimes exchange a few words with us in a guttural German accent. The pallor of the Balfours' faces was remarkable, but von Hügel's was of a deadly whiteness, and enormous, framed with white side whiskers. I thought that if ever I saw a ghost it would look like him. He and his wife Lady Mary, a Catholic convert, were an extraordinarily distinguished-looking couple, and we used to meet them at the early Sunday Mass at the Carmelite church – Lady Mary shuffling about in bedroom slippers with a slightly sideways gait.

Another celebrity to be seen sometimes in Kensington Gardens was Peter Scott – some seventy years younger than von Hügel. In those days when children wore several layers of woollen garments, beginning with combinations, he was conspicuous for being dressed like a child of the 1960s – no hat or socks, and shorts cut very high. His mother, wife of the Antarctic explorer, was a friend of the Balfours, and when Uncle Duggy once met him in the winter and asked him "Aren't you cold, Peter?" he answered: "Cold?" in a disdainful tone and whirled away on his scooter as if to say that, in his family, they were above such considerations.

During the war, when Rachel walked in the park, she noticed that whenever Millie and Eva saw Peter they said to each other "Look, there goes Captain Scott's little boy," and she thought how wonderful a thing it was to be a famous child; so as she went past groups of chattering nannies, she imagined to herself that they nudged each other and said

"Look, there goes the little girl who invented the tank."

At the bottom of Church Street the local suffragettes had their headquarters. These naughty grown up ladies fascinated us and we always asked to be taken past their office on the way home to read the latest slogan that was posted up in their window, with the vain hope of perhaps seeing a fight between a policeman and a suffragette with an umbrella. We had once been to tea with a wispy little lady called Maud, who had been to prison for setting some golf links on fire, and I had found it very hard to think of her or speak to her as an ordinary person. Here in Kensington ladies like her could be seen in a mass, dressed in strong coats and skirts and felt hats, marching up and down Church Street carrying their banners, with huge rosettes of yellow and purple pinned onto their chests.

IRELAND

Growing Up

EDWARDIAN parents seldom travelled with their children. I can only once remember as a little girl being in a train with my mother when, to my great pleasure, she took me on her knee by the open window because I felt sick. The really difficult journeys were left to other people. It was Nana who took us to Gruyère in 1909 and when we went to Ireland in the summer of 1913 our Swiss governess Mimjou, who spoke little English, was given full charge.

I spent the night before with Mabel Wynn, a friend of mother's, and Mimjou fetched me in the morning. She was late and very flustered. Mabel was a social worker, and the little house at which I stayed with her was in an out-of-the-way part of London; we had the greatest difficulty finding a taxi there and eventually made a mad rush to the station, to find that the guard was holding up the train specially for us. There he was, standing on the platform with Mother and Lily Tarver, his green flag ready, and we scrambled in at the door that he held open for us.

As the train chugged out of the station, Mimjou threw an unwanted coat into Mother's arms. She and Lily roared with laughter, but Mimjou didn't think it was at all funny and all the way to Fishguard she complained of having had to fetch me, until she saw the choppy sea, when she said "*Pauvres petits nous*," and concentrated on the crossing which was awful. Half way across the Irish Channel, Hester was heard to say "I shall never eat a banana again. I can swear to that."

From Wexford we took a slow train to Gorey, where a sidecar was waiting to take us to Cahore.

It had been decided that we should join the MacCarthys for the summer holidays, and Mother and Aunt Molly had taken a little house there called the Hermitage. The three MacCarthy children and their nurses were ready to receive us and we crowded in with them as best we could – it was far too small. When, a few days later, the two mothers arrived, very late, they hired a carriage at Gorey station and asked the driver how far it was to Cahore. He answered "Sure and if I were to drive you furiously through the night, we might be there within the hour."

They decided that the Hermitage was inadequate and appealed to the Anglo-Irish family called George from whom they had rented it. On calling at their house they were told that the mistress had gone out "in her hair," but, having found her, they arranged to rent a cottage and some lodgings in the village for the spill-over of relations and friends who wished to join us. Throughout the holiday there was a constant stream of uncles and aunts coming to spend a few days with us on their way to Dublin and other parts of Ireland. Among them was Aunt Valerie who brought her Russian maid, Varia, with her for the good of her health, and left her with us.

The sea shore was of sand with rocks and little bays and we had it all to ourselves. Varia used to go and find some deserted place on the rocks where she could undress and sit naked, singing Russian folk songs to the sound of the sea. When a coastguard saw her in the distance he went to warn her that she was breaking the law, but when he got near enough to hear her sing he was filled with awe and left her alone. (Poor little Varia died of tuberculosis in a London hospital soon after the Russian revolution.) When Stephen was at Cambridge in 1923 (where he was the only under-graduate reading Russian) he was travelling in Russia one summer vacation and was reminded of Varia. Walking on the shore of the Baltic, he came upon an old peasant woman sitting stark naked on the sand and singing to herself. He went up to her but she didn't notice him, so absorbed was she in her song.

While our elders enjoyed themselves travelling, we led a quiet nursery life with a daily bathe and an occasional tea party at the Georges' house.

We played in a little wood opposite the Hermitage where the trees were small and easy to climb. Rachel MacCarthy wasn't allowed into the wood because she talked too much, and that spoilt our games; so I used to crouch behind a bush

and roar like a lion to keep her away. Poor little Rachel stood in the road saying "I know it's you Clare. It isn't a lion. I can see you." But all the same she didn't dare to come any nearer.

When Uncle Desmond was at Cahore he enjoyed going for walks by himself. He came back late one evening full of enthusiasm for the long walk that he had taken along the sea shore which was quite deserted, for the tea that he had been given by a farmer's family, and for the talk that he had had with them.

After he had left my mother took the same walk and noticed on her way a thatched cabin standing alone on the grassy cliff above the shore. She went up and found that it was empty. There was a little pond nearby, a small hedged garden and several out-houses. There was no road to it – not even a track. She made enquiries and was told that the freehold value of the property was £100 or it could be rented out at £10 a year. She decided to take it for the following summer.

After spending the winter months in London we made the Fishguard-Rosslare crossing again in April, and went to a little port called Courtown, north of Cahore, to stay at the Taravie Hotel. This hotel was to have been called the Tara View, but when the china letters were unpacked, the W had been found broken, and they had never bothered to replace it. Taravie would do just as well, and the English tourists would think that it was an Irish word.

Here Aunt Margaret was waiting to receive us, sitting on her camp-stool doing water-colour sketches of the gorse and blackthorn blossoms, with Mount Tara in the background. It could be seen on most days across the bay, seeming to stand alone like an iceberg – a blue fairy-story mountain with a wealth of legend to it.

Courtown was a paradise, with its carpets of primroses

and long stretches of sandy beach covered with exquisite shells, and we felt as if it all belonged to us.

We had made friends the year before with the Comerfords who lived in a house called Levuka. Tom and Mary Comerford were a good deal older than us and Sandy and Dympna by a few years.

I had never before been into a house in which I felt so completely at home as Levuka. Mrs Comerford wore a felt hat on her head, rather like a man's, and walked about with her hands in her pockets. Though she had a weather-beaten appearance and looked older than she was, her relationship with young people was quite unstrained, and she mixed with them as though she was their age while still retaining authority. She and her children talked about their horses and dogs as though they were as important as people.

Mary was a splendid horsewoman and she kept her seat on a rearing horse with a calm smile on her face. She took me out riding every day, and I hero-worshipped her.

Unlike most parents my mother made a point of choosing fresh and bucking mounts for our first riding lessons because she said it would make us learn how to grip with our knees. Every time that I came back from a ride, Mrs Comerford asked me if I had been thrown, and I nearly always had; then she congratulated me, saying that it would make me into a good rider in the end.

Mrs Comerford ran a small school at Levuka with a Miss Brodie as governess.

There were three pupils of about Dympna's age: Moyra, Dorothy and Alice. Tom and Sandy Comerford were at a

Benedictine school nearby called the Mount St Benedict, with a Father Sweetman as headmaster, and two of the girls at Levuka had brothers there. These boys, and others at the Mount, often came to spend the day with the Comerfords.

When the Easter holidays were over, and David went back to school at Eastbourne, Hester and I stayed at Levuka as boarders while Mother was getting the cabin ready for us.

Mary took the history lessons – it was Irish history that was taught at Levuka – and catechism (Irish catechism). Moyra said to me one day "Do you not know when St Patrick came to Ireland? Are you not a Catholic then? 'Tis the first question of the catechism." But Mary was broad-minded about the catechism. When Hester and I showed her our books beginning "Who made you? Why did God make you?" she had to admit that the questions were more conducive to religious faith than the dates of St Patrick's life, and she allowed us to go on learning from them. Our catechism books had a crucifix on the cover and the Irish girls' a yellow harp on a green background.

The history lessons were made emotional by the presence of two English pupils and consisted of something more like a political speech than a lesson. After telling us about the iniquitous behaviour of England (past and present) towards the Irish, Mary would turn to us and say "Now you're ashamed, aren't you?" I didn't feel ashamed of my country because I never took in much of the lesson, but I did feel ashamed of my sister when she was reduced to tears; but these tirades in no way affected my relationship with Mary because there was no personal malice in them.

One evening after dark we went down to the little harbour to watch the youth of Courtown and neighbouring villages being given elementary training in drill. Instead of rifles they carried hurley sticks and garden tools. They were mostly barefooted and clumsy in movement, and the mock weapons often dropped from their hands. Among the crowd of onlookers I noticed Mrs Comerford standing with her hands in her pockets in earnest conversation with my mother. Did she foresee, then, how passionately her daughter would be involved in politics and how soon? Two years later, Mary was to make Irish history herself by taking such an active part in the rebellion that there was a price on her head.

When on the run she used to climb by the window into a flat in Dublin shared by Sandy and Dympna, to demand a suit of men's clothes and a hair cut. Once she was chased in a car by the Black and Tans and a bullet grazed her head, shooting off a bit of her scalp; she was as proud of that token of martyrdom as though it had been her first fox's mask and she nailed her own skin onto the wall above her mantleshelf with a long strand of hair dangling from it.

But all of this was later, and I was spared what would have been an intolerable division of loyalties. As it was I was proud to be her friend and favourite in spite of my nationality.

Miss Brodie's lessons were more professional. We read Beowulf and Chaucer with her and began some German. She made us do embroidery samplers and gave me ten out of ten for my drawing of the map of Ireland from memory.

When lessons were over we all ran down to the sea to bathe, sometimes taking the horses and ponies with us. With a lot of kicking and pulling we managed to get an occasional ride in the sea on horseback, and then Mary would hold onto the horses' tails to be towed.

When we were not on the beach we amused ourselves on stilts and became expert stilt-walkers, hopping up and down steps and dancing the polka on them; we threw stones from catapults cut from the hedges and fed our pets – each girl was allowed to keep one of her own. What a school it was!

All this time, Mother was making the cabin habitable. She had it re-thatched, and a road was built up to it across a field for the last quarter mile. Partitions were put up to make two little bedrooms, and it was whitewashed inside and out. She called it the Sheiling which, she was told, was the Gaelic for little house. The uneven floor was covered with matting, and the open fire was left as it was, with the wheel at the side to fan the peat from under the ground, and the thatch was left uncovered on the inside. Two outhouses were also whitewashed and repaired. A new gate

was hung at the entrance to the yard which was filled with shingle from the beach, and the little garden was dug.

An old tumbledown stable was repaired for Jessie the pony and her trap, and before we got to a main road we had to drive along our new little stretch of road to a track that was a mile long and divided by many gates.

When it was all ready and we went to live there, Hester and I drove to school at Levuka every day, while Stephen stayed at home to do lessons with Mimjou. Hester drove, and I got out to open the gates. She took the reins in chamois-leather gloves and imitated Mother's every movement as she drove. Hester assumed a lot of responsibility for which we should have been grateful but, far from it, we turned on her and said "Don't pretend to be Mother."

On that road we never met a single motor vehicle.

My mother had never cooked before but she had always

given the matter a lot of consideration, having a belief in good food, and she decided that, as she had succeeded in turning so many other people into good cooks, she could do the same with herself; so she plunged headlong into it without any preparations in the way of lessons and with the most primitive materials – an open peat fire and an oil stove in an outhouse across the yard. But with Mimjou's help, some cookery books, and long letters of advice from Belloc, she sailed away into her new-found talent as though she had cooked all her life.

The summer of 1914 was glorious, and we ate nearly all our meals out of doors in the shingled yard.

Lucky pre-war children that we were, we had never washed up before. It was such a new occupation that we thought it quite an adventurous thing to do, and special photographs were taken of us carrying the china to and from the outhouse.

Before leaving London we had been to tea with the children of some family friends who lived in a grand house. They also had a French governess who had said to Mimjou on hearing that we were going to Ireland *"N'est ce pas que c'est agréable cette vie de Château en Angleterre?"* Mimjou had agreed and kept her amusement to herself at the time, but she often laughed and reminded us of it as we did the washing up.

The rough work was done by a young boy with courteous manners called Hugh. He cleaned the saucepans in the pond with sand and dried reeds, and carried the water from a little spring on the side of the cliff; he groomed and harnessed the pony and cultivated the vegetable plot.

When Hugh was given his midday meal I couldn't resist staying at the door of the outhouse to watch him say grace. My presence gave him no sort of self-consciousness; he always took off his cap and made the sign of the cross before sitting down to his plate which he put on a packing case.

We took it in turns to fetch the milk from the farm which was kept by a family called Tomkins. This consisted of father, mother, aunt, and two children: Lizzie who was a good girl, and Richard who was a naughty boy. Good Lizzie stayed at home to work while naughty Richard came to play with us and to boast of what little he could, for instance "I'm after having a green box of matches." As for Miss Tomkins, she was a character, but a perfect pest. Her curiousity was so great that each of our visitors was forcibly engaged in conversation by her.

One evening I was sent to the farm to get some cream and the Tomkins asked me if I knew any songs, so I started off on 'The Golden Vanity' which we had been singing on the beach that morning. It was such a success that I was asked for another song and then for ballad after ballad, of which I had a large repertoire. As I was singing, and the story of the witch-mistress unfolded, Miss Tomkins interrupted me with "Sure and she must have been very wicked." But 'Rendall my Son' was not the last song, and by the time I was released to go home the meal was over and cleared away and the cream no longer needed. Everybody was very cross, and my excuse sounded very silly; I ate my remaining scraps alone.

On Sundays Jessie pulled us all to church at Bally Garret. The road was full of church-going donkey carts, zigzagging backwards and forwards, only our trap keeping to a straight course; but they were all going in the same direction until a crossing, where the Protestant donkeys' carts turned resolutely to the left.

On the way to Bally Garret we sometimes stopped at a tiny cabin by the roadside to visit an old woman called Marstella. Her conversation was supposed to be entertaining, but I was far too frightened of her to be amused and I thought that she must be a witch. When she delved among her clothes in a wooden chest to find some apples to give us, I didn't dare to eat mine for fear that it might be poisoned.

Marstella claimed to see many ghosts and she showed my mother the mark of a burn on her sheet from the hand of one that had appeared to her to say that he was in Purgatory.

Her mother appeared to her too, and the thought of anyone as old as Marstella having an even older mother (in this world or the next) terrified me – let alone their dialogues: "'Mother,' says I, 'When shall I be in heaven?'

"Marstella," says she, "in three years."

At half term my mother went to England to see David and Mrs Comerford came to stay with us at the Sheiling. We felt that she was our guest and in no way someone put in charge of us and she enjoyed the rough life, going for a walk by moonlight every night and only taking off her felt hat to sleep in the tent.

When Mother came back, a very long standing promise

was kept. I was at last to have a dog of my own. She had chosen me a black rough-haired cross-breed from the lost dogs' home because she liked the expression on his face which was miserable.

She had spent a night with him at Eton where the Vice-Provost had given him a Shakespearean name – Shough meaning mongrel – and by the time she got to the Sheiling he had become a one-man dog of the deepest dye and clung to her pathetically. It was thought that he might get attached to me if I fed him, but as soon as I put his dish down he stood over it and barked at me fiercely as though he had to defend his food. Nothing could persuade Shough that he was my dog. My mother complained of his habit of lying on her clothes while she bathed. I would have been delighted had he lain on mine and I tried to make him do so.

Shough wasn't half so much of a success as Hester's kid Pan, bought for a shilling out of a donkey cart, who followed her about bleating. Stephen was given a tortoise-shell kitten for his pet, but it never learnt the difference between the inside and outside of the Sheiling, and Mimjou said *"Quel petit chat ordinaire."*

One day Mother took me over to Mount St Benedict to have tea with Father Sweetman. She knew the parents of one or two boys at the school (a nephew of Maurice Baring's was there) and we were introduced to them. There were hunters in paddocks and stables and an Irish terrier bitch with a litter of puppies, and we were shown over the school buildings.

Father Sweetman was very anxious to have David and Stephen at his school; he had taken a fancy to them and said that they were just the kind of boys that he wanted. My mother told him that she had already made her plans for their education, besides which they were English boys; but it was English boys that Father Sweetman particularly wanted. This is hard to understand in the light of his later engagement in the Irish Rebellion, which was as wholehearted as Mary Comerford's. His commitment to the cause was evidently strong since he closed the school when he had the directive from Rome either to give up his political activities or to resign as headmaster. Mount St Benedict was a monastery and an offshoot of Downside. The school was of his foundation and showed every promise of success, but what he had built up he unhesitatingly allowed to go. After Home Rule was achieved he returned to the Mount to end his days as an ordinary monk.

I wasn't there on the day that he came to the Sheiling with Mr Franklin. I was out riding with Mary Comerford, but the others told me that I had missed something unforgettable, and they spoke of him as the perfect man. I have no idea who this Mr Franklin can have been – perhaps a young man who had just taken his degree and was thinking of teaching at the Mount – but I was given to understand that he was unique, and even Mother must have been struck by him because she thought that he might have fitted into a plan that she had long had in mind.

In Russia she had been much impressed by the standard of education of the children in the families she had stayed with; they were taught by resident tutors and had the early discipline of field sports and social life in their home, so she wondered whether boarding-schools were really necessary for the boys. Why shouldn't they travel abroad with a tutor? We might all go to Russia, and Mr Franklin would teach the four of us. But Father Sweetman's visits were frequent. He wanted my brothers for his school, and he pleaded and bargained with my mother so persistently that in the end she relented. David and Stephen were put down for the autumn term. The Mr Franklin plan might come off later.

There was a succession of visitors, and a tent outside the gate served as a spare room for those prepared to rough it. The less hardy friends stayed in Courtown and came to spend their days with us. Among them was Grandmama, the most appreciative of them all.

When Miss Margaret Parrat in South Africa had to fend for herself in a primitive village, Grandmama had written to encourage her: 'In all difficult circumstances remember the three things that I always say to myself, "I am an Englishwoman. I was born in wedlock. I am on dry land."' But when she saw her own daughter kneeling on the mud floor to cook over a peat fire, the primitive life seemed all romance to her, and those three things did not need recalling.

When she was with us, Miss Tomkins couldn't be kept away. She put on her best clothes and hat and covered herself with jet ornaments, and the two of them were a remarkable sight as they walked about the fields, Miss Tomkins leaning heavily on Grandmama's arm, saying "This is my favourite lady."

We had local visitors too. The Georges paid us a surprise visit from Cahore, smartly dressed and with veils over their faces. They could see nothing wonderful about living in a small cabin 'of clay and wattles made', and they walked about looking with curiosity into every corner. After asking a few suggestive questions about 'baths' they drove away in their carriage with their noses turned in the air, to everyone's relief.

A family called Donovan came to see us in a procession of carriages and bicycles, and we had a visit from a Lady Mary Doyne and her son Robin. Robin was as much of a success as Mr Franklin, and we talked about him for the rest of the holidays. What a lovely name it was, Robin Doyne, and he spoke of his bicycle as "My bike", which was so dashing.

Lady Mary sat with Mother at the top of the cliff dressed in a flowing blue linen dress, while Robin bathed and raced with us on thesands. He might have been fifteen and Hester was just thirteen, but I was aware of the flirtatious relationship that sprang up between them and felt rather proud of Hester. Perhaps she had been right when she told us that she had become a grown-up on her last birthday.

When Robin came to breakfast at The Cloisters later, he seemed to us just a correct Eton boy with sophisticated manners, and all the glamour had gone; but under the shadow of Mount Tara he was like a fairy prince.

Everything was different in Ireland and everything came off there. At Eton we would sit for hours on the banks of the Thames with grand fishing rods, only to catch a few minnows. David did once catch a funny pink fish with a smile on its face, a few inches long, but it plopped back into the river after jumping about in a jar that was much too small for it; but at Courtown we stood on a little pier with barefooted village boys, hauling in fish after fish, caught with a bent pin on the end of a string; and when we bought raffle tickets at the Bazaar we won the box of chocolates.

In Ireland, everything was romantic. The mushrooms grew in fairy rings and on the way to bathe we used to stop to look at a bright green frog that swam in a little gravelled basin of its own beneath a spring. Had he spoken it would have been no surprise.

Throughout that cloudless summer we never met a soul on the sea shore below the Sheiling. At every tide the waves laid a line of shells on the sand which we scoured, as we sang together, for those that were mother of pearl and for the many cowries.

Everything in Ireland was as it ought to be, and in the distance was Mount Tara of the legends, pure and pale blue, looking as though it had risen from the sea.

But as the summer advanced, Mother became more and more interested in the newspapers and impatient of any late delivery. She scanned the headlines anxiously and said from time to time "I say, you know! This looks serious!" And we would run away to play.

We were warned of the impending danger of war but we dismissed the matter from our minds. Everything was lovely in Ireland and we were there to enjoy it. What could war be like? It was impossible to imagine – so why think of it?

Then one day, when Hester and I were coming home, the wheel of the pony trap got into a rut; we turned over and Jessie fell. I jumped up and sat on her head to prevent her from kicking, and at that moment Lizzie Tomkins appeared, running towards us, and called out "War is declared, war has been declared!" So it had come at last, the dreaded news. Disaster was upon us.

There was a new look of anxiety on people's faces and Mimjou was less ready to laugh. She was thinking of her sister's husband in France. Mother was distracted and anxious to get home, also thinking of her brothers and many brothers-in-law (Uncle Christopher had died of wounds from the Boer War). For us it meant banishment – banishment from the paradise of Ireland and the paradise of childhood; and we had the fear of having to face up to an adult world for which we were not yet prepared.

That summer had been an enchantment, and as for the future, the former plans now sounded like the wildest daydream – a school to which you took your own pony and dog, where you hunted in winter and in the summer bathed in the sea on swimming horses, in touch with your own brothers at a school nearby, whom you met in the hunting field; and then perhaps to Russia with a tutor . . . Suddenly there was no future, the holidays had come to an abrupt end, and even Mimjou was leaving us. We pleaded with Mother but she was quite firm. In wartime one had to live in one's own country, and she refused to promise that we would come back to the Sheiling the following summer.

When we left, Shough broke loose to follow us, and I was made to get out of the trap to whip him away while he snarled savagely at me. I knew that it was my last farewell to him. Nobody had ever liked poor Shough and they shot him on some pretext soon after we had gone.

On the long drive to Gorey we were all very silent, until somebody had the idea of asking what we were each thinking about.

Hester was thinking of the novel that she was reading, *By What Authority* by Robert Hugh Benson, and David of the next Pierrot show at school; I was thinking about Shough. When it came to Mimjou's turn, she said sadly *"Moi, je pense à la guerre."*

THE BELLOCS

Cautionary Tales

IT was soon after my parents had settled at Ford in 1903 that they made friends with Hilaire Belloc. They were lunching at the Bridge Hotel at Arundel; *The Path to Rome* had not long been published and they were reading it with admiration. At another table a group of people were talking animatedly, dominated by a square-set young man with brown hair and very blue eyes. His voice was not loud but extraordinarily clear. My father and mother sat in silence and exchanged glances; they were enthralled by the torrent of wit and originality that poured from his lips as he darted from one subject to another. It could only have been the author of *The Path to Rome*.

A few days later he called on them in a pony trap, and a friendship sprang up that was to last for the rest of their lives. He wrote to them at this time: 'It will give me great joy to dine with you that night at your house which I think the most Sussex thing south of the Downs. I will bring along all my impedimenta and dress like a Christian.'

As a frequent guest at Ford he knew us all from our infancy: 'I have thought most carefully,' he wrote, 'of what the children would be most grateful for. I have some of my own so I can judge . . . I send a doll.'

The first time that I remember meeting Belloc was in London soon after his wife had died, in 1913, when I was nine years old. My mother and I met him after mass in Westminster Cathedral and walked with him to Victoria Station. He trotted along beside us with his tiptoe gait, dressed all in black with an Inverness cape and top-boots, and I was impressed by his look of great sadness and wondered how he could bear his widowhood. My mother was a widow, but I had the idea that it was far worse for a man.

Soon after this we went to spend the day with his children at his house in Sussex, and it made an enormous impression on us. We, who had lived at Dorking and in London and who spent our holidays abroad, had always longed for a country home, and King's Land was undoubtedly the house of anyone's dreams.

I was enchanted by its position on the corner of two small roads, by the rooms being level with the ground and opening straight onto yards, and by the sense of space that it was given by the long rambling passages and rooms on different levels. Then there were the farm buildings to one side, over which the sails of the windmill cast moving shadows as they turned round, and the stream that curled round the grounds with a footbridge over it leading to a long grass track that reached the Downs.

The house was a medley of grandeur and rusticity. French and English furniture was combined there in every sort of style. On the walls hung good and bad pictures, family portraits, landscapes and photographs, with a crucifix over every beam 'so that the infidel should have to bow his head', and the little chapel upstairs was covered with holy pictures, souvenirs of shrines, and mortuary cards of friends.

The house was run by the Sussex-born maidservant, Edith, who had the beauty of an English milkmaid and cooked like a Frenchwoman, serving the meals as though King's Land were a grand country house. Old English china and French family silver, beautifully polished, were laid on a long refectory table that shone like a mirror and stood on the uneven stone floor of the dining room.

On arrival we were greeted by the youngest child, Peter, who was about my age, with a large and shaggy dog called Big Jaws. He took us to see a little rusty stove under a walnut tree that he had lit with some sticks and on which he was cooking some weeds. Then, one by one, the others turned up – Louis the eldest, Eleanor (then fourteen), Elizabeth just back from a ride on the pony called Sir Edward because he was grey, and Hilary who was twelve.

King's Land was the house of our dreams, but we soon discovered that companionship with the Belloc children was strenuous and alarming. They were given a freedom that few children were allowed and they took advantage of it to the utmost. Their father's idea was that human life is so vulnerable, and happiness so rare and fragile, that they should be encouraged to enjoy themselves as much as possible in youth. As they liked risking their lives, travelling by rail without a ticket was one of their pleasures; the country trains were boarded at a bound outside the little railway halts as they gathered speed. The boys showed us a hole in a field caused by the explosion of a mine they had made themselves; and what other children that we knew so much as dreamed of possessing invisible ink?

Instead of the innocent games that we played, like 'Poor Archbishops', we were introduced to one of their invention called 'The Terrible Death'. For this my brother Stephen was chosen as a victim. He was put into one of those reservoirs on wheels that were used for watering gardens; Hilary and Peter Belloc lifted him into it, and when he crouched down his white head just peeped out of the top. Then they rushed him down a slope into the duck pond where he remained splashing backwards and forwards in the levered tank until some kind volunteer came to rescue him. There were plenty of volunteers to wade in in their clothes – even in mid-winter the Belloc children walked through the flooded fields up to their waists in water.

Stephen, being the youngest of us all, was always the one chosen to fill whatever receptacle formed the focus of our games. Once when we were staying for our holidays in a flat at Littlehampton, the Belloc children put him into a tradesman's lift at the back of the house and hauled him with the rope to an upper floor, where an angry old woman

opened a window, and there they left him for a tête-à-tête with her for as long as it amused them to do so.

The Terrible Death was not so bad, but I knew that Peter had been let down the well in a bucket during one of these

games and I had the haunting fear of this being done to me or to Stephen.

Then there was the windmill which soon changed from a picturesque spectacle into an arena for feats of courage, far beyond the daring of us timid Balfours. When the miller was away and the sails were at a standstill, Elizabeth used to climb up them, carefully placing her feet between the shutters; and when the sails were in motion, Louis lined us up on the narrow platform half-way up and made us rush across it between each swirl of a sail. As the sails circled inside the wooden rails of the balcony, the game was very dangerous. From the top of the windmill a cat had once been made to take a leap, tied to a parachute made to its size by Louis, and from here, too, the flying capacity of the hens was tested. I never liked to stay up at the top for long in case I was coerced into some similar flying experiment.

We would be called in from these alarming outdoor games by Edith for lunch in the tiny schoolroom, where the nine of us sat round a small deal table – but eating a meal certainly did not mean peace. Hilary would take some gunpowder out of his pocket, lay it in a trail from plate to plate, and set it alight. Or it might be Louis' turn to cry out "Hell!", at which the Bellocs would all take up their steel knives and grate them on their plates to simulate the sound of gnashing teeth. Meanwhile Mr Belloc and Mother would have gone down a long passage to disappear into a sacrosanct part of the house behind the many green baize doors that had been put in for silence at the time of Mrs Belloc's last illness.

When we stayed at King's Land, Hester and I slept with

Eleanor in a large four-bedded room next to the chapel, and here we sometimes played a game that the Bellocs called 'The Pleasures of the Poor', which consisted simply of a clandestine midnight feast celebrated in nightgowns and pyjamas while speaking in cockney accents.

When Edith had gone to bed, Elizabeth would come to us from her own room and the boys would creep downstairs to raid the store cupboard of tinned foods and biscuits and fetch a tin-opener and a few spoons; then we all sat on the floor to tuck in. Because food has the same effect on children as alcoholic drink and instantly increases their vitality, the feast would be followed by a rough pillow fight. When the noise of our voices rose, Mr Belloc would call to us from a distance, producing a sudden awful silence: "My children, you make too much noise." Eleanor would shout back "We were only talking Papa." "It is late my children. You must go to sleep." "Yes Papa."

After this interruption we continued to indulge in The Pleasures of the Poor whilst speaking in a whisper.

Mr Belloc had a great admiration for my mother as an educator and hoped that she might be able, in some ways, to lessen the loss to his children of their own mother. But although she was intimate with Eleanor and Elizabeth they always called her Mrs Balfour, and I think the boys found her rather alarming. However, Peter once gave her, as a birthday present, a purse filled with shillings, since whenever his father came to our house on one of our birthdays he counted out shillings into our hands up to the number of years we had attained. Peter couldn't run to my mother's thirty-five-odd years, so as her birthday fell on

September 8th he put eight shillings into the purse.

Our parents had the idea that their two families would benefit by contact with each other, so we were constantly thrown together and this was resented on both sides. The Belloc children had a code of their own and it had to be followed. They made us feel fools, and we hated their way of continually challenging us, and pulling our legs. When Michael MacCarthy was taken out sailing in the *Nona*, they had told him that the sails were made of sailors' trousers, and I never knew when to believe their yarns. Their French republican spirit and criticism of the existing social order was something quite new to me. We had always got a lot of enjoyment from imitating the cockney accent and Irish brogue, but it had never occurred to me that our own accents could be caricatured until I heard it done by the Bellocs. When we went to a meet they talked loudly about the 'dogs' and their 'tails' and the possibility of the fox going 'down a hole' in aggressive derision of the conventions of the field.

We were all much the same age, but in many ways I felt as if the Bellocs were far older than us. Louis and Eleanor once had a long argument which filled me with amazement. Eleanor had read Rudyard Kipling's poem 'If' and had been inspired by it.

> If you can meet with Triumph and Disaster
> And treat those two impostors just the same.

"It's so true," she said, "because they are impostors, aren't they?" I was trying hard to understand what the passages she quoted were all about, and the discussion, as it went on, led me into a labyrinth of bewilderment. Louis said that 'If' was priggish, boy-scoutish, public-schooly and full of the spirit of British Imperialism. Now, what was wrong with the boy scouts, that worldwide organisation? Public schooly! Eton was a public school, and Louis was at Downside: wasn't that a public school too?

As for the spirit of British Imperialism, I couldn't imagine what he meant by that.

Then one day when my mother spoke of a mutual friend who had lost her son, Eleanor said "Poor woman!" with feeling, and I wondered how she could know what it felt like to be the bereft mother of a child as old as us. For me a bereavement was something embarrassing, to be quickly forgotten.

Elizabeth, a little older than me, was my favourite. She had brown curls hanging round her pale face down to her shoulders, and I admired her chaste appearance as much as her keen enthusiasm for life and her response to the romantic. Eleanor told me of how she had once had a bad cut in her hand and had said nothing about it; she was found by chance holding it under a cold tap and on the verge of fainting. Louis had rushed off to the doctor on his bicycle to say, "Come quick, my sister is bleeding to death," but the accident was kept from her father. I thought that this was admirably brave.

The same stoicism was shown another time by Hilary when he was suffering from a bilious attack. There was no question of his staying at home or of telling anyone that he felt ill. He should have been in bed, but he came out with us all on a picnic party, frequently and discreetly being sick so that his father shouldn't notice.

I always enjoyed Elizabeth's companionship, but she had a way of suddenly disappearing into an intellectual world where I couldn't follow her. In the evening at King's Land, when Mr Belloc relaxed after his work and played cards and paper games with his children, choosing the easier ones so that the conversation could be kept flowing, Elizabeth never took part; she was always curled up in the corner of the French Empire sofa reading a book – not of the kind that I used to read by O. Henry or Mark Twain, but nearly always the life and letters of some literary person of whom I hadn't even heard.

Peter, on the other hand, seemed to be engaged in reading *King Solomon's Mines* for most of his childhood, speaking the words to himself and moving his finger slowly across the lines to keep his place. His father used to call to him from the card table: "What's that you're reading, my child?"

"*King Solomon's Mines*, Papa."

"Have you got to the crunching of the bones?" (with the French guttural r).

The answer was always "Not yet, Papa."

It is sad that Elizabeth's gifts never fulfilled their promise. Only two small volumes of her poetry were published and they were hardly noticed. The following is from a long poem called *Pelion*:

> O first and dearest,
> Did no man warn you
> That friend and brother
> May live to mourn you?

> Did no man tell you
> O light heart ranger,
> Of cliff and thicket
> Alive with danger?

The last verse goes:

> I told you this
> When we sat together
> By the centaur's fire,
> In the winter weather.
> I made an arrow
> So sharp to handle
> And you stooped over
> To mend your sandal,
> And bound it tight
> With a thong of leather
> In Chiron's cave
> Where we sat together.

When my mother was engaged in conversation with Mr Belloc, I was very disconcerted. Politicians for whom I had heard the Balfours profess the greatest respect – they might even be family friends – were spoken of either as scoundrels and racketeers or as gaga old fools, and the British Government described as an organisation forever engaged in hatching plots to deceive the sheep-like masses.

When it came to the Catholic Church, as it so often did, there was always an obstreperousness in his apologia as he thumped on the Catholic tub. Under-statement for him was a form of cowardice.

This intransigence applied to everyday things as much as to religion. Unpunctuality was counted as a criminal offence; there was just as much vituperation over margarine and Cerebos salt and many other things to do with cooking and wine as over heresies. He obstinately refused to have the telephone at King's Land till the end of his days, and no hedge or tree that his wife had planted was allowed to be cut down. But as to the practice of religion, he liked the simple approach and what is called 'nursery Catholicism'. Whenever we went into a church with him there was a lot that he liked to do. He put up candles to his favourite saints and kissed St Peter's toe and stuffed coins and notes into all the little boxes – St Anthony's Bread, Peter's Pence and the Holy Souls – all the things that were branded as superstitious.

We often spent part of our holidays at Littlehampton and then he would bring his family over in the rickety Ford car to make an invasion into our tame lives.

He and my mother stayed at home to talk while we went off to bathe, but the Bellocs' idea of bathing was terrifying. The beach was much too dull for them; they liked to swim across the Arun, from one jetty to another, however fast the tide was running. If it was going out there was a possibility of being carried out to sea, which they found exhilarating, and if it was flowing in, they allowed themselves to be carried far up into the town; and for them it was a pleasure to walk shockingly through the streets in dripping bathing dresses. They were once reproved by a policeman for doing so and astonished him with their eloquent repartee.

Mr Belloc sometimes kept his sailing boats at Littlehampton – the *Nona* and what he called 'the other boat – a sort of Noah's ark, big enough to hold tribes of children,' the *Dreadnought*. After a lot of persuasion he managed to overcome my mother's reluctance, and she agreed to let him take us all in it for a short cruise along the coast to Shoreham.

We were eight children and, in all, a party of eleven including the boatman, so the *Dreadnought* was greatly overloaded. We were told that the Littlehampton bar was particularly hard to cross, that the boatman had been especially engaged on this account and would go ashore in a dinghy as soon as we had got out to sea, and that it was important that we children should keep as quiet and as still as possible.

We were crowded into a small and stuffy cabin. I always felt seasick on these expeditions and was haunted by the fear of actually being sick, and the atmosphere very soon became oppressive. We sat in two rows with our legs stuck out straight and our shoes in each others' faces, while the boat swayed backwards and forwards. Then we heard yells and shouts and swear-words addressed to the boatman, and the clattering of feet above our heads. The *Dreadnought* had got stuck.

There was a rushing from one side of the deck to the other as she was pushed over with a boathook, first this way and then that. I thought how awful it would be if I were sick all over those sixteen legs. If I could have some fresh air it might be avoided!

Then Hilary said quietly "The centreboard is down." Eleanor called up to her father "Papa! The centreboard – '' but before she could finish her sentence she was shut up. "Keep quiet, my children. You must be quiet. This is a very difficult operation." After a little more rolling backwards and forwards, we decided that Hester should act as inter-mediary, and she tried to get in touch with Mother to tell her of the situation, but again the order came from the deck "Keep quiet, my children. I must have you quiet." So the rolling went on and became almost unbearable, till Elizabeth said "Let's pull the centreboard up ourselves". It wasn't easy to do in such cramped quarters, but we managed, and the *Dreadnought* immediately took to the water and went smoothly over the bar; the boatman was sent off, and we sailed out to the open sea. At last we were allowed up on the deck, where we listened to Mr Belloc telling Mother about the difficulties of the Littlehampton bar, and what skilled navigation it required. The fresh air was welcome, and Mr Belloc asked us to sing him a song that he particularly liked:

> 'Tis Mr Doodley
> 'Tis Mr Doodley
> And without a man like him what should we do?
> It's education
> That makes the nation
> Says Mr Doodley-oodley-oodely-oo.

I never felt at ease on these trips. In addition to the seasickness, there was no freedom to be enjoyed. I can't remember ever being reproved by Mr Belloc, but I once heard him say to a boatman with vehemence, "There's not the slightest use in being sorry", and I lived in fear of his displeasure whenever we were out at sea.

This incident of the crossing of the bar gave me a profound insight into the working of human affairs: the men at the top rushing about in noisy agitation, giving the wrong orders and silencing good advice, the boasting of what had really been done by an inferior below deck, secretly and efficiently, with no fuss and no reward.

One Easter holidays when my mother rented a cottage on Exmoor the Bellocs joined us, staying in a nearby village. David, Stephen and my mother were already at the cottage when Hester and I went to spend the night of Holy Saturday at King's Land, to motor down the following day. A Franciscan priest was staying there too and said mass in the chapel before we started off on our long drive.

Mr Belloc was in splendid form as he had just broken his long Lenten fast from alcoholic drinks and he sang old French hymns and English music-hall songs all the way to Exmoor. One minute it was:

> Venez divin Messie
> Sauvez nos jours infortunés

and the next:

> My old man was a fisherman
> He might have been a militia man . . .

We were six children squashed into the car with a huge pile of luggage at the back, and we nibbled Easter eggs all day. By the time we had reached the West Country, the Ford had had quite enough, and it wasn't equal to the steep hills. The petrol tank was right at the back and couldn't feed the engine on a sharp incline, so that we often had to get out and push. This was fairly easy. What was far more difficult was holding the car back going downhill when the brakes began to fail.

We were going round a hairpin bend when Mr Belloc called out "Make an act of contrition my children!" and his hat flew off as he drove the Ford with a crash into a wall on the far side of the road. We all got out to pull it back into position, and our progress downhill continued in slow stages of about twenty yards, after which the car got out of control, dragging a row of children behind when Mr Belloc turned it into a ditch, and operations had to begin all over again.

The last miles of the journey were complicated by the radiator continually boiling. Mr Belloc warned us that this was dangerous, and gave us instructions on how to jump out if the engine should seize up. Luckily that country is full of streams, and we were able to fill the radiator frequently. Whenever he sighted water, Mr Belloc gave a shout and stopped the car, and we all tumbled out of it to rush to the stream, fetching water by whatever means we could – Hilary and Peter filled their scarlet school caps, and Elizabeth scooped some up with half of a chocolate Easter egg; I got hold of a cardboard Easter-egg box.

While this improvised fire brigade operation was in progress, a man on horseback in a smart riding habit went by and laughed at the sight; and it was a long time before we shook him off. He caught us up as we went downhill, going in and out of the ditch, and he overtook us as we pushed the Ford uphill, and his derision became more and more insolent, till we managed to outride him on a comparatively flat bit of road, when Mr Belloc raised his hat and bade him farewell with excessive courtesy. We arrived at nightfall in a state of utter exhaustion.

Here in Devonshire we felt superior to the Bellocs and got a little of our own back. Exmoor was more beautiful than their Sussex Downs, and stag-hunting a superior sport to their tame fox-hunting. Mother had been born at Lynton and we were ardent patriots of the West Country. But here again, as at Littlehampton, we found ourselves behaving with a wildness that was not really in our nature, and when the Bellocs were there I felt like a stranger in my own country.

At the time that I first remember Mr Belloc, he was beginning to make money from his writing and revelling in his new affluence, giving presents on all sides. At Christmas he liked to take us all to the pantomime in London, and we were generally crowded into a box from which we could hardly see between each other's heads. He enjoyed the jokes and horse-play as much as we did. One year the show was *Red Riding Hood*, and Stanley Lupino took the part of the Grandmother, Widow Twankey. We watched him slowly undressing on the stage to hoots of laughter from the audience, taking off a pair of bright red stays and looking under the bed before getting into it. When we came out, Elizabeth told me she thought that he had gone too far. "It was perfectly clear what was implied," she said. (This must have been at a suburban theatre. A West End producer would have had to consider the sensibilities of a genteel audience.)

But even in those days of opulence not a penny was spent on appearances. Belloc still drove about Sussex in the shabby old Ford, calling on even his smartest friends in it – to their embarrassment. Sometimes it was filled to overflowing with noisy children sitting on the hood and mudguards; sometimes Belloc's friend Father Vincent MacNabb would be sitting beside him in his white Dominican habit – a very unusual sight before the First World War and, incidentally, still against the law then. The Belloc children wore clothes that were patched and darned by the hard-worked Edith, and the girls' summer dresses were generally faded and too short; but they had wonderful presents. When we went back to King's Land one Christmas holiday, our mouths watered at the sight of the cameras, binoculars and bicycles that their father had given them. Hilary had a magnificent football, and as we played a wild and shrieking game with it in a field, Wilfrid Scawen Blunt* drove up with a lady beside him, sitting erect in a phaeton drawn by two Arab horses.

He came into the field and stood beside Belloc to watch us. The two men were both Sussex-born, both cradle Catholics, both unsuccessful Liberal politicians and both poets. In appearance they made a striking contrast – Belloc short, stout, clean-shaven, dressed all in black, and Wilfrid Blunt with a grey beard, magnificent in stature, tall and thin in a long yellow checked coat that came down to his ankles.

Belloc only needed to see some genuine quality in a person – innocence of any kind especially – to become lastingly attached to them. I remember his saying that he liked the society beauty as a type of woman because she had the innocence of a spoilt child. He enjoyed the company of the aristocrat because of his insistence on gaiety and his nonchalance; but though he was glad to move in high circles he wrote to a friend in middle age: 'I am tired of being the rich man's buffoon'. He was extraordinarily affectionate, and he wrote to my mother when we were grown up: 'My children were children with your children, and this makes me feel very close to them.' And again: 'I

*Wilfred Scawen Blunt, 1840–1922, traveller, writer and breeder of Arab horses.

saw Clare in Paris. I wouldn't like to miss a chance of seeing any of your children. I have a special fondness for each one.' Desmond MacCarthy used to say of Belloc that he was the most misunderstood of men, that too many people were put off by his aggressive self-assertion and too few appreciated his clarity of vision and the depth of his humanity.

King's Land has remained in the Belloc family, unchanged. It is the only house I know that has remained exactly as I knew it in childhood, sixty or seventy years ago.